The Language of News

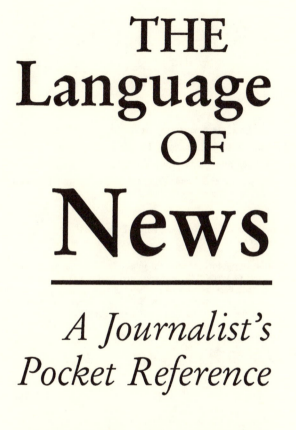

THE
Language
OF
News

*A Journalist's
Pocket Reference*

JACK BOTTS

Iowa State University Press / Ames

JACK BOTTS is professor emeritus at the University of Nebraska-Lincoln College of Journalism. He was a reporter and editor for 17 years before beginning a 24-year teaching career at Nebraska, where he was sequence head and News-Editorial Department Chairman for 18 years.

© 1994 Iowa State University Press, Ames, Iowa 50014

☺ Printed on acid-free paper in the United States of America

First edition, 1994

Library of Congress Cataloging-in-Publication Data

Botts, Jack.
    The language of news: a journalist's pocket reference / Jack Botts.—1st ed.
        p.   cm.
    Includes bibliographical references and index.
    ISBN 0-8138-2494-X
    1. Journalism—Style manuals. 2. English language—Usage—Handbooks, manuals, etc. I. Title.
PN4783.B68 1994
808′.06607—dc20   93-29910

Contents

2 Common Language Blunders

3 Usage

4 The News Story

Preface

This volume grew from decades of perception that both practicing and student journalists need a handy reference on the language and writing as it applies to them.

For 17 years as a newspaper reporter and copy editor, and 24 years as a professor of journalism, I found weaknesses almost daily in standard and academic references.

Individually, most dictionaries, academic grammars, reporting textbooks, stylebooks and books on usage are complete. But most aren't written for journalists. Few come in simple, practical form. Few combine grammar, language faults, usage, spelling, story blunders and basic style references.

While journalists and student journalists normally find reference works available in newsrooms and classrooms, they obviously don't use them often enough. Questioned about the quality of their writing, some journalists try to excuse their work on the time and effort required to find an appropriate reference.

Such excuses seem only marginally valid, but one objective of anyone directing or teaching journalists should be to remove both real and imagined barriers.

Months of search through standard reference works helped me to eliminate and select subjects. A 42-year collection of semi-organized notes helped me to focus on material peculiar to journalistic needs. Every note and memo regarding common language faults helped me to select useful guidelines. Years of service on Associated Press Managing Editors Writing and

Editing Committees gave me hundreds of examples for raw material. Editors throughout the nation may recognize some of their examples taken from wire stories.

I developed definitions and guidelines in the usage section from *Webster's New World Dictionary* and a consensus among H.W. Fowler, Theodore Bernstein, Roy Copperud, Rudolph Flesch, Wilson Follett, James Kilpatrick, Michael Swan and Rene Cappon. Failing any consensus I relied on my own practiced ear.

Some readers may think it absurd to include a review of basic grammar. Terms like "predicate nominative" alone can send shudders through healthy bodies. But those same readers will think it absurd that most grade school, high school and college students have never studied grammar nor have most of their teachers. Journalists need grammar, despite some educational theories to the contrary.

Three old American-written volumes proved especially useful in tracing the direction and development of grammar and writing for the past 140 years. When dealing with a changing language it pays to learn what changes have proved to be important and what have been unnecessary baggage.

Once settled upon, guidelines had to include examples, clear, precise and appropriate to journalistic writing. Standard reference works too often offer pages of examples that a journalist would never write. To fill the reality requirement most examples passed through several revisions. Similarly, to be included in the usage section and spelling list, words also had to endure the test of common newspaper use. My definitions do not include the strange and exceptional.

In Parts Two, Three and Four, especially, examples come directly from faulty sentences, leads and stories saved from classrooms, newsrooms and newspapers. My only changes have been in time references and proper names to avoid disconcerting former colleagues and students.

This volume concerns writing and not reporting, but

readers will find a few references to reporting, especially in Chapters 15, 16 and 17, where each affects the other.

I wish to thank those fellow journalists who actively or unknowingly contributed examples. I especially wish to thank my wife, Dorris, for lending her ear at crucial points and for her patient support while these pages were under way.

This effort will have been worthwhile if the volume survives the test of all such work: daily use by journalists who care.

The Language of News

1

Review of Grammar

1

Why Study Language?

There was a writer named Nell,
Whose words rang true as a bell.
She wrote what she meant,
And the message she sent,
The audience understood well.

Actions and Words

We often say that actions speak louder than words. That makes some sense, but think about it: nothing happens without words, before, during and after the action. Words can speak more precisely than action, and words may well determine the nature of action. Whether we have peace or war, love or hate, creativity or waste, can depend on our choice of words, our language. Conversely, actions influence our words, so the two become interwoven in all our lives.

Some people hold positions that give their words influence over the actions, the lives, of many of us, even whole communities, nations and the world. These people often head governments or institutions and industries, but not all of them. Some of the people whose words influence the lives of others are journalists. Their words, written or spoken, carry the actions and words of others to large audiences. Their choice of words, and their general ability to use the language, determines how well they convey the world's news to their audiences.

All that sounds relatively simple from such a broad perspective, but the best journalists have learned at some pain that the English language makes its own hard demands. It dances with a writer in sheer delight one minute and in the next kicks the would-be wordsmith in the pants. Our language insists that writers choose words and build sentences precisely if a story is to paint a faithful picture.

Some who call themselves journalists never learn this about language and the news. In their writing they continue for years to throw ill-chosen words and unsound phrases at audiences, hoping apparently that some, like mud, will stick. Some who claim the title of editor pass such writing on without regard for reader comprehension, attending only to the most obvious mechanical errors. In defaulting a crucial responsibility they not only serve their craft poorly, they deny themselves the excitement and enrichment that dedication to language can give their lives.

Writers and editors of news deal most importantly in information. Both work in the middle, between the actors on the world stage and the audience. Most people in this audience are not in a position to witness the words and deeds of the actors. The old newsreel motto, "The Eyes and Ears of the World," hints of the responsibility placed upon journalists. If they write and edit responsibly they try faithfully to ensure that bits of information pass through them intact from the minds of the actors to the minds of the audience.

Deplorable things can and do happen to news in its passage from sources to readers and viewers. However, information overlooked or misinterpreted because of poor reporting, while of primary importance, is outside the scope of this discussion. Here the emphasis will be on preventing misunderstanding and distortion in news by using accurate language in writing and editing.

Proper language by a journalist entails the use of some long-respected rules and guidelines. We all appreciate that the

English language continues to grow in expression because we don't strangle it with rules. We should also recognize that rules or guidelines in grammar and punctuation give the users of English a common workbench and common yardsticks on which to base understanding.

A currently popular trend in English instruction plays down most language rules as inhibitors of expression. That approach, while of doubtful value even in English classes, is absurd for anyone who intends to receive and transmit information with precision and accuracy. That approach can create chaos when the information involves matters of peace or war, life or death. We all enjoy discussing what a popular author meant by using these or those words in a novel. But consider the frustration which results when a news story forces one to ask what the writer meant, even in one sentence. Communication of information won't allow us to abandon rules that enhance meaning.

Inaccuracies in facts can destroy the credibility of any news organization, but so can carelessness and inaccuracy in language. Why should any reader yield time and attention to a writer who shows little working knowledge of the language? While the journalist's audiences may be amateurs in regard to many of the facts, we must assume that readers and viewers know something about their own language. If they discover lapses in spelling, grammar, word usage and phrasing, they're likely to question the writer's accuracy with the facts as well.

English, the most widely spoken language in the world, has acquired the largest vocabulary of all, perhaps two million words. Half of the world's books are written with those words, and about 80% of all computer text is stored in English. If that recital gives you a warm feeling that the world has found a perfect tool for communication, cool it. Although we profess our love for English and for the noble literature recorded in our language, it's far from foolproof. Good writers ennoble the language. Unwary or careless writers fall victim to its weaknesses and faults. They also weaken the language by adding to those faults.

Journalists regularly write or recite what has been called the "first rough draft of history," but if they read widely, they should know how unreliable, illogical and downright deceptive their words can be. Unless they choose words with precision and build phrases carefully, they can confuse or mislead more than they inform. Without constant attention users of the English language can stand reason on its head. For now it's enough to say that many words have two or more meanings, and that most things or acts find expression in several words. One expects some lunacy in a language's idiom, but those looking for consistency or logic in English spellings, sounds, verb tenses, parallels, opposites and even rules, may easily consider their language a lost cause.

Then why try to make sense of it or to follow its rules? Because it can be the most adaptable, most expressive and most effective tool a writer could desire. English can provide grace to any feeling, a word of the right nuance for any purpose. It offers a selection of verbs to describe any action precisely. It presents an infinite range of sounds, rhythms and patterns which, in the hands of someone who cares, can bring tears to the eyes and wonder to the brain. As a journalist's major instrument it can wrap news in brilliant clarity and sense.

It can. But the English language doesn't give up its beauty and its depth to passive, casual study. It rewards the serious and the patient, those students of language who always try to improve and who place the audience and the audience's understanding first.

Methods and Messages

Far too many news organizations, writers and editors seem to place other objectives ahead of their audiences. Writers often seem to write for editors. Editors seem to edit for other editors or for publishers. Publishers seem to publish for advertisers. Whole newsrooms seem to plan their work more to accommodate electronic gadgetry and beautiful "packaging" than to present the news clearly to the audience.

All writers, editors and publishers must wear the reader's shoes every minute if they truly want to be journalists. They must ask themselves constantly, "Is this as clear and simple as we can make it?" They can't allow electronics or "packaging," as marvelous as those may be, to get in the way of news, to become ends rather than means. The best electronic systems in the world won't make a semi-literate reporter seem literate. The most beautiful colors and newspaper layouts won't put the right words before the audience.

Assuring the clarity of news messages requires hard, patient work, and attention to the right objectives. It's frustrating to try to hire and train people who can write and edit news that an audience can understand. It's hard work for news desk chiefs to demand good writing, to figuratively sit on their reporters' shoulders until they get it. But it pays off. Readers may not flood the mails with their congratulations, but even if they don't completely understand why, they'll feel better about their newspapers. Even more important, they'll read more news and gain a better understanding of their communities and their world.

2

A Brief Review of Grammar

There was a young writer named Danner
Whose words he hit with a hammer.
He told us off-hand
"Who cares where they land?
My talent was never in grammar."

Consistency and Growth

Most journalists have had to give some attention to rules of English and especially to grammar if only to be consistent. The publishing world, including newspapers, is built around consistency, so it demands the framework the rules provide. Journalists also should value the satisfaction that comes from developing a sure hand and sure ear for the right words. Nobody can survive long in a modern newsroom without the ability to write in complete and somewhat intelligible sentences. Still, though all journalists should always try to write as well as possible, their language talents range all the way from stumbling to sparkling, even in the biggest and best newsrooms.

News and copy editors, who presumably have an edge in those skills, quickly learn to recognize writers who grasp grammar and are building their language skills and those who probably won't improve because they don't work at it. Strong reporting somewhat counterbalances habitually weak writing and vice versa, but journalists who don't try to develop their writing through grammar skills usually don't improve their status. They'll stay at the same positions for years, inflicting faulty prose on their editors, and worse, on their readers. Often without knowing it they join in a dubious crusade that is killing English grammar.

Mastering the rules of English grammar shouldn't overwhelm a journalist who understands how vital it is to do so, both for career success and effective communication. It takes time, attention, and especially practice to make words work as they should in the world of communication.

It may mean developing an "ear" to recognize the sounds of English words and phrases when properly or improperly used. That takes constant writing and reading to understand one's own weaknesses and to learn how others use the language, even those who use it ineffectively. All this writing and reading should be critical, challenging every word and phrase for clarity, usage and placement. Discovering that an effective writer sometimes breaks a rule of grammar should spur the reader to learn why and how such rule-breaking works. It won't spoil the pleasure either of writing or reading to question words or construction. It should become a life-long habit. If this kind of writing and reading takes a little longer, one can charge it on the ledger of self-education.

In studying grammar, as with any other complex subject, it helps to start with the parts it deals with.

Parts of Speech

To understand the ways words fit and act together, students of language have tried to separate them into categories. These attempts haven't always been successful, but they have provided a useful framework for studying and improving word use and sentence structure.

The most dependable way to determine a word's part of

speech is to ask how it is used in a sentence. That often means disregarding the form of the word, because that same form can appear as more than one part of speech.

Nouns

Nouns name a person, place, thing, idea or quality.

A *proper noun* names a specific person, place, thing, etc. Examples: Bill Jones, Kansas City, Mount Everest.

A *common noun* names members or individuals of classes of persons, places or things. Examples: man, city, mountain, apple.

A *collective noun* names a collection or grouping instead of an individual person or object. Examples: council, band, troupe, brigade, flock and so forth.

An *abstract noun* names an idea, quality or state. Examples: love, truth, walking, soreness.

A *compound noun* unites two or more words. Some may start as two words which gradually combine into one. Some pass through a stage of hyphenation. Journalists must decide if they are two words, hyphenated, or one word. The dictionary provides the best authority. Examples: light bulb, post office, horse-trader, porthole.

Nouns can change their forms in four ways: in *number*, in *gender*, in *person* and in *case*.

Pronouns

Pronouns are the most common words used instead of a noun. The noun a pronoun stands for is called its *antecedent*. A pronoun must agree with its noun antecedent in case, gender, number and person. Like nouns, pronouns can be used as subjects of sentences, direct objects, indirect objects, appositives, or objects of prepositions.

Personal pronouns follow their antecedent nouns. Examples: I, you, he, she, it, one, we, they. (*It* and *they* can be *impersonal pronouns* when they don't refer to people.)

Compound personal pronouns can refer to the same person as the subject, as *reflexives*, or emphasize a preceding substantive, as *intensives*.

> She injured *herself*. (reflexive)
> I *myself* saw it. (intensive)

It's a common error to use the reflexive *myself* where the sentence needs the objective case *me*, especially when the object of the preposition is doubled.

> He gave it to John and *me*. (Not *myself*)

Demonstrative pronouns refer to a specific person or thing: this, that, these, those.

Indefinite pronouns refer to a person or thing less definitely than a demonstrative pronoun: one, some, someone, each, either, all, few, several, many, etc.

Relative pronouns can refer to an antecedent and connect a dependent clause (also called a relative clause) to a main clause: who, which, that, what, as, whoever, etc.

> The house *which* he entered had been offered for $80,000. (In addition to referring to the house, the pronoun connects it to the rest of the sentence. *Which he entered* is the relative clause.)

Writers should remember that the proper relative pronoun is *that, which* or *what* if the antecedent is an animal, a thing or a collective noun for a business, association or governing unit. The proper relative pronoun is *who, whom* or *whose* if the antecedent is a person or an animal with a name.

Interrogative pronouns (who, which, what) are used in asking questions: *What* happened to the ball?

Reciprocal pronouns show mutual action or relationship: *each other, one another.*

Adjectives

Adjectives modify (describe, limit and qualify) nouns, pronouns or other adjectives.

Descriptive adjectives are the most familiar to us: the *bumpy* street, the *white* flower, the *tangled* fish line.

Predicate adjectives come after linking verbs (forms of to be, appear, become, feel, grow, look, seem, smell, sound, taste) and refer to the subject: The water was *cold*. The room seemed *small*. The bell sounded *dull*.

Articles are the adjectives *the*, *a* and *an*, which precede the noun or pronoun they describe and are notable because they don't compare. *The* is called the *definite article* because it refers to a particular person or thing. *A* and *an* are *indefinite articles* because they refer to one of several similar persons or things. *A* is proper to use before a word that begins with a consonant sound, and *an* is proper to use before a word that begins with a vowel sound: *a* theater, *a* history, *a* hemisphere, *an* apple, *an* idea, *an* honest man.

Proper adjectives are proper nouns being used as adjectives: *Chinese* restaurant, *Mount Wilson* Observatory.

Verbs

Verbs provide the action for a sentence, telling what the subject is or does. Sentences with strong verbs give writing power and description. Every verb has *person, number, tense, voice,* and *mood.* They are *regular* or *irregular.* Verbs can be *transitive, intransitive* or *linking.* They also can be *main* verbs or *auxiliary* verbs.

Main verbs stand alone or appear together with auxiliary verbs.

> He *saw* the officer. (*Saw* is the main verb.)
> He *has seen* the officer. (*Seen* is the main verb and *has* is the auxiliary.)

Transitive verbs have an object that receives the action of the verb.

> She *wrote* three sentences. (The noun *sentences* forms the object of the verb *wrote*.)

The object may be a pronoun and may even appear before the verb. It helps to be able to identify it as the object of the verb in order to determine its correct *case*:

Whom did she interview yesterday? (*Whom*, the *objective case* of the pronoun *who*, is needed here because it is the direct object of the verb *did interview*. To identify it, one may have to rearrange the sentence mentally: She did interview *whom* yesterday.)

Intransitive verbs don't take a direct object. They may be *linking* verbs and take a predicate nominative or a predicate adjective, which can be confused with a direct object.

> He *is* a pilot.
> This *is* he.
> She *will be* dressed.

Or they may be complete verbs, taking neither an object nor predicate complement.

> The woman *slept*.

Adverbs

Adverbs modify verbs, adjectives or other adverbs. They can introduce sentences, connect independent clauses, or modify whole phrases or sentences. They can state degree, time and manner. They can be classified as *simple, interrogative, conjunctive* or *sentence* adverbs.

Simple adverbs come directly before or after the word they modify.

Police officers moved *quickly* to the scene. (modifies the verb *moved*)

We watched a *slowly* developing storm. (modifies the adjective *developing*)

Interrogative adverbs ask questions.

Why are the taxes so high? (modifies the verb *are*.)

Sentence adverbs, instead of connecting one clause to another, modify their sentences. Those most frequently used are: *sincerely, honestly, personally, regrettably, frankly, to be honest, to be frank.*

It's a common error to use *hopefully* as a sentence adverb. It should be a simple adverb, meaning *filled with hope*, as in "He started his new job *hopefully* and energetically." Instead, careless writers use it this way: "He said that *hopefully* he would finish the book tomorrow." That's faulty because it doesn't indicate clearly who's hoping. Instead, write it: "He said he hopes to finish the job tomorrow."

Conjunctive adverbs act as connectors or transitions from a dependent clause to an earlier clause. They can come at the beginning, in the middle, or at the end of a clause. Here are some of the more common.

also	in the first place
anyhow	meanwhile
besides	moreover
consequently	nevertheless
for example	on the other hand
furthermore	otherwise
however	still
indeed	therefore
instead	

Here's an example.

> She washed her car *although* she knew it would rain.

Prepositions

Prepositions start phrases and show a connection between the noun or pronoun that follows and other words in the sentence. Many idiomatic expressions in English depend for clarity on the precise choice of preposition. Prepositional phrases often take the part of adjectives, or adverbs, describing where or when.

> The shelf *under the desk* held the forms. (as an adjective modifying *shelf*)

> Sentences *in the book* were too long. (adjective modifying *sentences*)

> He went *down the road* to the store. (adverb modifying *went*)

> It rained *throughout the day*. (adverb modifying *rained*)

Idiomatically, prepositions also can be parts of verbs: *look up, head off, carry out, look into, pick up, take off, try out*. In such cases, consider the preposition an integral part of the verb.

Conjunctions

Conjunctions connect words, phrases or clauses.

Coordinating conjunctions (and, but, for, nor, or and yet) connect words, phrases or clauses that are of equal weight grammatically.

> Cheese *and* crackers (connects words)

> Through the woods *or* down the lane (connects phrases)

He bought his tickets, *yet* he couldn't board the plane. (connects two independent clauses. Note the comma before the conjunction.)

Correlative conjunctions, like coordinating conjunctions, connect words, phrases and clauses of equal weight, but they come in pairs: *either . . . or, neither . . . nor, as . . . as, as well . . . as, if . . . then, both . . . and, not only . . . but also, not so . . . as, whether . . . or*, etc.

Neither brown *nor* green appeared in the painting.

He looked *not only* in the cupboard *but also* under the stairs.

She is *as* intelligent *as* she is resourceful.

Subordinating conjunctions, such as *whether, if, though, since, although, until, because, as* and *while*, connect two unequal segments of a sentence. Usually this conjunction connects an independent clause and a dependent (subordinate) clause that modifies it.

The snowstorm hit the area hard *because* nobody had prepared for it.

Because they introduce dependent clauses subordinating conjunctions need not be set off with commas.

Interjections

An interjection is an exclamatory word or phrase used independently in a sentence.

Gee whiz! Whoopee!

3

Dealing With the Parts

───────────────────────────────────

There was a young writer named Brown,
Who knew how to write for renown:
"It helps in a fix
To learn all the tricks
And to tell a verb from a noun."

Sentences

It helps to consider a sentence as one unit of language and composition, an expression of a complete thought. A sentence has at least one independent clause and may have several dependent clauses. By creating clear, forceful sentences a writer can use words to produce varieties and combinations of ideas limited only by knowledge of the subject.

Clauses

A clause is a group of words with a subject and predicate. If it can stand alone and express a complete thought, even qualify as a sentence, it is called an *independent clause*. Even with subject and predicate, however, if it doesn't express a complete thought, it's a *dependent clause*.

John gave his lunch to the squirrel (complete, so an *independent clause*)

19

after he ate the hamburger. (incomplete, so a *dependent clause*)

Combining these two clauses could easily form a sentence of an independent clause and a dependent clause.

John gave his lunch to the squirrel after he ate the hamburger.

Phrases

A *phrase* contains a group or groups of related words but lack a subject or a predicate, or both.

on the waterfront, sitting in the sand, after the concert, in trouble again

Parts of a Sentence

Any sentence can be reduced to two primary parts: its *subject* and its *predicate.*

The subject, a noun or pronoun and usually before the verb, is the actor or being of the sentence, the part that answers the question, "Who's doing it?" or "What's there?" It may have a modifying word or phrase with it.

The *shortstop* threw the ball to first base. (The actor)

The white *house* sat alone on the lonely hillside. (Thing)

The predicate is the verb part of a sentence, expressing the action or state of being. It may be a single word or a complex grouping of modifiers, objects or complements.

One journalist covered the early primaries. (*Covered* is

called the *simple predicate,* and *covered the early primaries* is the *complete predicate.*)

A *direct object* is part of the predicate and receives the action of the verb. It answers the question *who?* or *what?* the verb is acting on.

> The quarterback threw the ball to the receiver. (What did he throw? The *ball.*)

> Sunshine gradually warmed the spectators. (Whom did it warm? The *spectators.*)

An *indirect object* is the person or thing to whom or to which, or for whom or for which something is done. It is an indirect object, in fact, if one can place *to* or *for* in front of it.

> He gave me a book. (Although *book* is the direct object, *me* is the indirect object.)

A *predicate objective* (sometimes called objective complement) simply restates the direct object in a different word.

> The president's wife christened the ship Mayville. (*Ship* is the direct object. *Mayville* is the *predicate objective.*)

The *object of a preposition* follows a preposition and is a noun or pronoun.

> He went into the *office* and looked behind the *files.*

> The blanket under *him* gave protection from the cold *ground.*

Predicate nominatives and *predicate adjectives* are nouns, adjectives or other parts of speech substituting for other words and coming after a linking verb. They describe or define the subject.

> It is *I*.

> The snow became *slippery*.

> Nothing had been *decided*.

Nouns of direct address state the proper name of the person addressed.

> That's the seat, *Mary*.

> *John*, we're over here.

Appositives rename a person or thing just named. They could take the place of the noun or noun substitute they follow, but are considered adjectives.

> The helmsman, *Poirot*, gave the ship a southerly course.

> The parrot, *the bird with the broken beak*, chattered noisily.

A *subject of an infinitive* appears just before the infinitive and just after the verb.

> A vote canvass showed *her* to be the winner.

> The forecast indicated *March* to be the wettest month.

An *object of an infinitive* answers the questions: who? where? or what? after an infinitive.

> They asked her to send my *book*.

Johnson wanted me to enter the *race*.

An *object of a gerund* is the noun (or substitute for it) after a gerund:

Raking *leaves* all morning left him hungry.

He couldn't settle for eating *apples*.

An *object of a participle* is the noun (or substitute for it) after a participle.

Receiving her *card*, he felt better.

He could be found watching a *movie* on most afternoons.

Idioms

Idioms are expressions that have become accepted in the language even though they often make no literal sense and defy rules of usage and grammar. Most originate in common experiences. They are peculiar to their language and carry the authority of popular approval. They are phrases that follow you home and live with you. They can be overused and become cliches. Here are examples:

having a bone to pick	to take a walk
to get in hot water	nip and tuck
to throw in the sponge	to put your foot in it
with a grain of salt	to make a bee line
riding a high horse	to stick by one's guns
the fat's in the fire	hard and fast
let the cat out of the bag	to play second fiddle
strike while the iron's hot	take the bull by the horns
to break the ice	in the same boat

to mince words   by hook or crook
to stand to reason   a stiff upper lip
cart before the horse   under false colors
too many irons in the fire   put best foot forward
the wrong side of bed   birds of a feather
hit below the belt   turn over a new leaf
get a handle on it   hold your horses

4

Forms of Nouns and Pronouns

There was a writer named Ward,
Whose phrasing won no award.
His editor got drastic
And fed him some plastic.
His tales now sell by the yard.

Subjects, Objects and Substitutes

A noun can form the subject or object of a sentence. It is a person, place, thing, idea or quality. Other words, pronouns, gerunds, or infinitives, can substitute for nouns, as can whole phrases or clauses. A word or phrase has taken the place of a noun if one can substitute a pronoun for it. Any word or collection of words used as a noun is called a *substantive*.

Proposing a new leader came hard for him.

He was resigned to *giving it all he had.*

Case

In changing case, nouns and pronouns alter their form according to their use in sentences. The three forms of case are *nominative, objective* and *possessive*.

Nouns change only in their *possessive* form, by adding *'s* onto a singular noun and *'* onto a plural noun in most cases, but stylebooks allow for several exceptions, largely because of common usage and to avoid awkward constructions.

Here are a few simple rules to help sort out the exceptions.

1.   Add *'s* if the singular noun doesn't end in *s.*

He filled the *desk's* drawers.

2.   Add *'s* to a singular common noun that ends in *s,* except where the next word begins with *s,* in which case the writer adds only the apostrophe. The rule applies even to those words ending in *s sounds* and avoids the sense of tongue-tangling while reading.

the *mistress's* book....but the *mistress'* stationery

the *quince's* taste....but the *quince'* seeds

3.   Add only an apostrophe to a singular proper noun ending in *s.*

James' house   *Illinois'* roads

4.   Add only an apostrophe to nouns appearing in plural form even though the meaning is singular.

mathematics' equations   *Boy Scouts'* rules

5.   Add *'s* to any plural noun not ending in *s.*

workmen's compensation   *media's* explanation

6.   Use the correct possessive form for the possessive nearest the noun where there is shared possession.

John and *Mary's* apartment

Jim and *James'* trail

7. Use the correct possessive form for each possessive when possession is separate.

Illinois' and *Iowa's* roads

8. Use the correct possessive form for the part next to the possessed noun when dealing with compound construction.

the Highway *Department's* schedule

her sister-in-*law's* dress

Choosing the correct *case* for pronouns can cause the most difficulty. Between these two examples, which should a writer choose?

It was *her*.

It was *she*.

Answer: It's *she* because it follows a linking verb, making it a predicate nominative, which must appear in the *nominative* case.

Similarly, a pronoun that is the subject of a sentence, even if those parts of the sentence are in compound form, must be in the *nominative* (sometimes called *subjective*) case.

He ate the apple.

He, she and *they* all appeared at the gate.

Which form would the writer choose between these two examples?

He thinks the same as *me*.

He thinks the same as *I*.

The good writer would choose the second. The sentence should be completed mentally, in which case it would read: He thinks the same as *I do. I* is clearly the subject of a clause, and therefore must be in the *nominative* case.

If a pronoun is the *direct object; indirect object; object of a preposition, participle, gerund or infinitive; or the subject of an infinitive* it must be in the *objective case.*

Which of these examples would a writer choose?

The teacher gave the book to *him* and *me*.

The teacher gave the book to *he* and *I*.

Answer: Make it *him* and *me* because they are both objects of a preposition and must be in *objective* case.

Here are other examples where one needs the *objective* case.

The teacher helped *her*. (direct object)

The teacher gave *him* the book. (indirect object)

Seeing *her*, the teacher entered. (object of participle *seeing*)

Teaching *her* is enjoyable. (object of gerund *teaching*)

The teacher thought *her* to be *me*. (*her* is subject of infinitive to be; *me* is object of infinitive to be)

If a pronoun is to show possession it must be in the *possessive case* form.

my, mine	his	one's
our, ours	her, hers	their, theirs
your, yours	its	whose

Which of these two examples does a writer choose?

The editor supported *his* buying the book.

The editor supported *him* buying the book.

Answer: Make it *his,* because a pronoun followed by a gerund should be in *possessive* case.

Gender, Number and Person

Most writers have little difficulty with gender, number and person of a pronoun once they are certain of its antecedent.

Gender of pronouns is so apparent from their form that mistakes appear only where there appears to be a choice, as in *neither . . . nor* constructions.

Which of these examples would a writer choose?

Neither Sally nor Jim would pick up *his* camera.

Neither Sally nor Jim would pick up *her* camera.

Answer: Make it *his.* The noun following *nor* determines both the gender and number of the pronoun.

Nouns change number (to plural form) in most cases simply by adding *-s* to the singular form. Nouns ending in *s, sh, ch, x* or *z* need an *e* to make the plural pronounceable: *axes, marshes, irises.*

Nouns ending in *-y* preceded by a consonant usually change the *y* to *i* and add *-es: armies, skies, flies.* Nouns ending in *-y* preceded by a vowel usually add only *-s: boys, bays, plays.*

Nouns ending in *-fe* change the *fe* to *ve* and add *-s: knives, wives.* Nouns ending in *-f* vary so much in the plural that one should check a dictionary when in doubt (note loaf: *loaves,* but chief: *chiefs*).

Nouns ending in -*o* preceded by a vowel add only -*s: folios, radios, cameos.* Nouns ending in -*o* but preceded by a consonant vary so much the dictionary should settle one's doubts. Here are some examples.

> autos, bamboos, dynamos, pianos, quartos, solos

> echoes, heroes, mosquitoes, tomatoes, torpedoes

The following irregular plurals of nouns follow no rules because they have survived from old English noun forms.

> brethren, children, deer, feet, geese, mice, men, sheep, swine

Compound nouns usually make plurals by adding -*s* or -*es* to the important word in the compound.

> courts-martial, passers-by, sons-in-law

But if parts of the compound noun are closely joined and taken as a simple word, the plural is usually formed at the end.

> handfuls, cupfuls

Number in pronouns causes problems only in trying to remain with singular forms and thereby running onto the shoals of sexism.

How would a writer choose among these examples?

> A renter should check *his* keys.

> A renter should check *their* keys.

Renters should check *their* keys.

Answer: It's best to choose the third example, the plural form. The first choice, *his,* is sexist, and the second is not grammatical.

The *person* of pronouns causes problems only in a lack of consistency in the use of *one.*

Which example should a writer choose?

When *one* starts this project *one* needs a clean desk.

When *one* starts this project *you* need a clean desk.

Answer: Choose *one.* When the antecedent is *one* the pronoun also should be *one,* and not *he, she* or *you.*

5

Verb Characteristics

There was a writer named Burr,
Who in mastering mood caused a stir.
He thought the subjunctive
Fell short of constructive,
Be that as it may, as it were.

Distinguishing Verbs

Verbs can be described according to their *number, person, tense, voice, mood, transitiveness* and *intransitiveness*. Any one of these distinguishes the individual verb and its choice in good writing.

Number

A verb corresponds with the subject of its sentence in number. Careful writers keep in mind the *number* of the subject, even in complex sentences. One source of confusion arises because, although nouns (often the subjects) usually add *-s* when plural, plural verbs often drop the *-s*.

Person

Verbs don't appear to have person because they don't change much as they are paired in conjugation with all the persons of pronouns. Usually, only the third person singular form changes, as in I *sit*, you *sit*, he *sits*, we *sit*, you *sit*, they *sit*.

Tense

Tense in a verb indicates the time of the action. Although some students of grammar would contend there are more, six *tenses* for each verb are enough for most writers to put to work.

Present tense indicates a present action or states a general truth: I *write;* you *write;* he, she, it, one *writes;* etc.

Past tense indicates an action or state in the past: I *wrote;* you *wrote;* he, she, it, one *wrote;* etc.

Future tense indicates action yet to come: I *shall write;* you *will write;* he, she, it, one *will write;* we *shall write;* you *will write;* they *will write.*

Present perfect tense indicates action that began in the past but continues to the present: I *have written;* you *have written;* he, she, it, one *has written;* etc.

Past perfect tense indicates action that was completed before some other past action: I *had written;* you *had written;* he, she, it, one *had written;* etc.

Future perfect tense indicates an action that will be completed before some other future action either mentioned or implied: I *shall have written;* you *will have written;* he, she, it, one *will have written;* we *shall have written;* you *will have written;* they *will have written.*

A writer must observe the sequence of time in tenses and make certain that verbs in dependent clauses conform to the verbs in the main clauses. In many news stories it's important to maintain tenses consistently. Exceptions are stories in which the time of actions shifts through past, present and future almost from paragraph to paragraph. Some feature stories and magazine stories make use of a *flashback* technique in which the writer must shift from the *past* tense to the *past perfect,* then to the *past* again.

Voice

Verbs are in either *active* or *passive* voice, the form which indicates whether the subject acts (*active*) or is acted upon (*passive*). Anyone who seeks force and directness avoids *passive* verb forms because they are wordy and weak. Also, passive sentences often omit the phrase telling who did it.

Which of these examples would a writer choose?

The attendant *was shot* (by the holdup man).

The holdup man *shot* the attendant.

Answer: The second, active voice, example not only is direct, but tells the reader who did it.

Passive verbs fill technical, scientific and even some scholarly writing to describe what the author *did* rather than to involve the author constantly as the *actor*. Journalists sometimes must use *passive* voice when the *actor* is unknown or unimportant, and the action or object of the action is more important.

Three hundred and fifty soldiers *were wounded* in the first three days. (The *cause* of war wounds is diverse and difficult to determine.)

Mood

If it were not for all the errors committed in the stumbling search for the right mood of a verb, most students of English would rather forget it. Of the four moods, however, only one, the *subjunctive,* sometimes seems unnatural to the ear and causes problems. Writers can train their "ear" by reading the work of good writers so that even the subjunctive is natural. (Note the subjunctive *were* in the first sentence of this paragraph.) The others, *indicative, imperative* and *conditional* moods, are common and fall naturally into speech and writing patterns.

Most sentences in English are in the *indicative* mood, meaning that they state facts or ask questions directly.

I *wrote* the letter.

Whenever a sentence includes a command or a request or provides instructions it's in the *imperative* mood.

> *Take* the ball.

> *Let's take* the ball.

> *Please take* the ball.

> *Start by driving* two miles south.

Whenever a sentence provides a condition, it's in the *conditional mood* and requires one of the four conditional verbs to accompany the regular verb. Note that the verb forms expressing the conditional mood in the second column below don't express the certainty of the verbs in the first column:

I can go	I *could* go
I shall go	I *should* go
I may go	I *might* go
I will go	I *would* go

Because many writers don't use or don't know how to use the *subjunctive mood,* the proper verbs don't appear as often as they should in English.

If used correctly, the subjunctive verb form *were* often appears somewhere after *if* in sentences whose main clause is in the conditional mood.

> Helen said that if she *were going* she *would be* dressed.

Which of these examples would a writer choose?

> Jane said she wished she *were* in school.

Jane said she wished she *was* in school.

Answer: Make it *were*. In expressing a condition that isn't true (a hope, a doubt, a prayer, a wish, even a request of desire) a writer needs the *subjunctive* mood form.

When using the present tense of the subjunctive mood a writer turns to the infinitive form without the *to:* I *be,* we *be,* you *be,* he, she, it, one *be,* and they *be.*

The driver asked that the six gallons *be* added to his bill.

The present tense of the subjunctive mood varies from the same tense in the indicative mood only when expressing the third person singular.

We proposed that the baritone *sing* (instead of sings) the third part.

The subjunctive form of the verb *to be* is always *were* in the past tense. Most problems in using the subjunctive show up with that verb, so one should develop a feeling for the right sound. The subjunctive verb form appears in several English language idioms: so *be* it, far *be* it for me, God *be* with you, *be* that as it may, *come* what may, long *live* the king, would that it *were,* etc.

Regular and Irregular Verbs

A verb is called *regular* if it forms its *past tense* or *past participle* by adding *-ed, -t* or *-en:*

wade . . . waded   sleep . . . slept   ride . . . has ridden

A verb is called *irregular* if it forms its *past tense* or *past participle* by changes in the middle of the word, as in *bear, bore, borne; drink, drank, drunk.*

Transitive and Intransitive Verbs

Verbs are called transitive or intransitive in sentences depending upon whether they have a direct object, the receiver of the action. A verb may appear in one sentence as transitive but in another as intransitive.

Which of these verbs would a writer choose?

The announcement *dived* stock prices.

The announcement *dropped* stock prices.

Answer: Choose *dropped* because it is a transitive verb and therefore will take an object of the action (stock prices). *Dived* is intransitive, meaning it will not take an object. (One cannot *dive* anything.)

But note that the verb *dropped* also can be intransitive:

The stock prices *dropped*.

One form of intransitive verb appears to take an object but doesn't. Such *linking verbs* simply connect a subject and a noun or pronoun to affirm or describe.

John *is* a pilot.

In addition to all forms of the verb *to be*, these intransitive "links" include *become, act, continue, grow, remain, stay, seem, feel, taste, look, sound, smell* and *appear*.

Regular intransitive verbs do not take an object or link a subject to a noun, pronoun or adjective.

The swimming teacher *dived* into the pool. (*Into the pool* is an adverbial phrase modifying *dived*.)

He *slept* loudly at times. (*At times* is an adverbial phrase modifying *slept*.)

She *dreams* every night. (*Every night* is an adverbial phrase modifying *dreams*.)

Verbals

Verb forms sometimes become other parts of speech. These *verbals* appear in three varieties: *gerunds, infinitives* and *participles.*

Gerunds

The present or past participial form of a verb that is used as a noun is called a gerund.

Writing provides practice and discipline.

Three children were among the *rescued.*

Any noun or pronoun coming before a gerund should appear in the *possessive case.*

His *opponent's swimming* gave him an edge in total points.

Participles

The present or past participial form of a verb that is used as an adjective is called a participle.

Writing with an objective, he soon completed the story. (*Writing* modifies *he.*)

We saw a house *standing* on a hill, *unpainted* and *untended.* (All three words modify *house.*)

Infinitives

As a verb form an infinitive usually appears with a *to* in front of it, not as a preposition but as part of the infinitive. Infinitives can take the place of nouns

> *To write* is to feel satisfaction and achievement.

and can be used as adjectives

> The manuscript *to sell* is the one just completed.

or as adverbs.

> He started *to wash* his car.

6

Point, Counterpoint

There was a writer named Gray,
Who threw all his commas away.
He said in frustration,
"I've failed punctuation.
Now tell our readers to pray."

Why Punctuate?

Punctuation makes sense of our thoughts. It isn't a mechanical requirement as some writers may think, but one inherent in language. Erected as a courtesy by writers, these highway signs offer readers a path clear of obstacles. Because punctuation signifies the relationship of parts of a sentence, mastering it presupposes a knowledge of grammar. Understanding the functions of words, phrases and clauses makes the purpose of punctuation marks clearer.

For consistency and success good punctuation requires agreement among its users, something it rarely has had. Exception after exception in newspaper stylebooks undermine agreement, and books on grammar rarely concur on all matters. Credit the Associated Press for years of effort to eliminate in its stylebook many of the senseless differences that for decades separated newspapers and news agencies.

Full Stops: Periods, Question Marks and Exclamation Points

These three marks are easiest to remember and use. They all signal the end of a sentence and normally don't cause a writer problems. All bring the reader to a stop but in different ways, according to the writer's purpose.

> She is here.

> She is here?

> She is here!

News editors, weary of struggling with long and windy stories, often wish reporters would find the period key earlier in their sentences. Writers who don't understand the proper use of periods, however, usually don't last long. Modern stylebooks make clear how periods should be used with abbreviations.

Which of these examples would a writer choose?

> She asked why she had to appear?

> She asked why she had to appear.

Answer: The second example, because question marks shouldn't appear after indirect quotations.

Note that verbs like *asked, wondered* and *questioned* make the interrogative aspect clear. Also, journalists should never insert a question mark to label their own irony or humor.

Exclamation points rarely appear in newswriting, so they scarcely require attention. They may mean that the writer has been forced to alert the reader to an excitement that the words can't produce on their own.

Commas

Commas cause more problems for writers than all other punctuation marks, probably because so many of the rules are wobbly. Some editors imagine that their writers sit at the keyboard with a handful of commas, scattering them like flowers in a garden. Other editors wonder if their writers have any commas in supply at all. Many writers follow a useful sense that a comma ought to go wherever a pause is indicated.

It's best to learn the hard-and-fast rules about where to use and where not to use commas, then develop and trust a good sense for other occasions.

Where to Use Commas

1. To separate items in a series

> He said he likes sailing, fishing, hunting and hiking.

Note the absence of a comma before the conjunction *and*. Use a comma before the conjunction when sentence construction makes it necessary.

> The children played softball, cops and robbers, and cowboys and Indians.

2. To separate two independent clauses connected by a coordinating conjunction (*and, but, or, nor, yet* and *for*)

> Police officers arrested three men on the corner, and a squad car pursued a woman in a small van.

3. To separate an introductory clause or phrase from the main clause

> Early on Tuesday, the president boarded a plane for London. (after an adverbial phrase)

Waiting for the ambulance, John interviewed the investigating officer. (after a participial phrase)

Because the weather became threatening, the Coast Guard issued a small craft warning. (after a dependent clause)

4. To set off inserted, nonessential words, phrases or clauses, even proper nouns

No, John, the book hasn't arrived.

The Wilsons, his party-loving neighbors, decided to build a patio.

The Brandenberg Tigers, a team that never lost during the season, won its tournament finale.

5. To separate coordinate adjectives. The test is whether the adjectives can be interchanged and can be separated as well by *and.*

They took the short, direct route to town.

Adjectives that indicate age or color aren't coordinate and don't require commas.

6. To separate the adverbs *too, as well* or *also* when they appear at the end of a sentence

In this instance it was better to sing, as well.

7. To separate *said* from the quotation it introduces, if the quotation is one sentence long:

During the session the mayor said, "The budget has all of us worried."

8. To set off such conjunctive adverbs as *however, therefore, likewise, at the same time*

> He decided, therefore, to add another course.

9. To set off the abbreviation for a state when it appears after the name of a city, and after the year when it follows a month and date

> The general arrived in Salina, Kan., on July 23, 1992, just before the ceremony.

10. To separate the abbreviation *etc.* at the end of a series

> The Jeep brought everything available: ammunition, overshoes, canvas tarps, etc.

11. To separate duplicated or similar words

> Whatever he did, did this mean his ordeal was over?

12. To separate thousands, in figures greater than 999.

> 1,234

Note these exceptions: years (1992), street addresses (1234 Adams St.) broadcast frequencies (2220 kilohertz).

Don't Use Commas

Commas should be inserted to improve readability and understanding, not to obstruct it. So don't use a comma

1. To separate a trailing dependent clause

> The company commander decided to fall back because his men were exposed. (*Because* introduces the dependent or subordinate clause and needs no comma.)

2. To separate parts of a compound adjective where a hyphen works best

> He dug three holes in the copper-brown dirt.

3. To set off a quotation from the following part of a sentence when the quotation ends with a period, question mark or exclamation mark

> "What do the voters want?" the mayor asked.

4. To set off a partial quotation or indirect quotation

> The candidate reddened at what he called "blatant insults."
> He said he wouldn't repeat the words used.

5. To separate two adjectives when the second adjective is more closely connected to the noun modified

> The new coffee filter

> The last evergreen tree

6. Outside quotation marks. Periods and commas always go inside the quotation marks.

> "The mayor will join us later," the chief said.

Semicolons

The semicolon isn't used much in newswriting. Journalists prefer complete stops and starts rather than something halfway between a comma and a period. They'd rather break two independent clauses into two sentences with a simple, clear period than join them with a semicolon.

One practical use for a semicolon is to add clarity when setting off parts of a series that also contain commas.

> The ex-governor is survived by his wife, Julia, of Elmwood; a daughter, Dana, of New Orleans; and two sons, James of Omaha, Neb., and George of Des Moines, Iowa.

Colons

The colon offers a formal way to introduce, present or announce lists, quotations, and even dialogue or sentences.

> The battalion commander prepared his battle plan: shell the enemy into submission, attack with all companies abreast and mop up remaining strong points.

> The Senate published a laundry list of objectives: a new tax plan, a space budget, a farm program and an immigration quota.

> The Council put these prices on street projects: $750,000 for Center Street, $450,000 for Harrison Avenue and $800,000 for the new Newton interchange.

> The mayor said one word described his reaction: shame.

Use a colon to introduce a quote of more than one sentence. Any complete sentence after a colon should start with a capital letter.

> The governor said: "State taxes won't stand further tinkering. Legislators need to go home. Taxpayers will simply have to tighten their belts."

Use a colon also to separate chapter and verse in a biblical citation (Exodus 3:6) and to separate the hour and minutes in references to precise time (12:34 p.m.).

Some techniques in publishing interviews make good use of colons to show questions and answers, or responses when two or more people are being interviewed.

> *Q:* Did you accept the check?
> *A:* No. Only the list of names.
>
> *Johnson:* My tax plan is ready for consideration.
> *Ward:* I'll have a proposal by next week.

Some newspaper copy desks allow the use of colons instead of *says* in headlines, but the technique is overused, and in many cases it's questionable whether the reader understands who's talking.

Dashes

Journalists have been accused of using the dash out of laziness in mastering more formal punctuation. Whatever the reason, the dash has gained in use and acceptance, probably because of its simplicity and clarity in some applications. It can lose its effect, though, from overuse, and it can intrude where other punctuation works better.

The dash works well in the middle of a sentence, introducing a group of elements that are separated by commas.

> All the Air Force's elements—the strategic, tactical and transport commands—became involved within a week.

Quotation Marks

Journalists must exercise care in using quotation marks. Here are the important rules:

1. Place quotation marks around only the newsmaker's precise words and make certain they are in full context. Readers should be able to tell which words are the speaker's and which are supplied by the reporter.

> "This is the worst crash scene I've ever worked," the officer said. He blamed thrill seekers for interfering with rescue workers.

2. Place semicolons and colons outside the quotation marks.

> The assistant said, "The governor won't approve it"; leading legislators only shrugged.

3. Place question marks and exclamation points inside quotation marks if they are part of the quotation, but outside if they aren't.

> "Who asked that question?" the mayor asked.

> Can we go to see "The Farmer's Daughter"?

4. As a general rule avoid placing quotation marks around brief phrases or single words. The only excuse for this practice is to enclose colorful or distinctive expressions. The danger lies in taking those words out of the context in which they were uttered. Readers may suspect the reporter's motives for singling out specific words.

> The mayor said the "agreement" didn't mention solutions for the budget problem. (This may imply to readers that the mayor doesn't like the agreement.)

5. News writers should never insert their own attitudes or opinions by gratuitously placing quotation marks around words. First, this practice confuses readers, who may assume the words

came from one of the persons being quoted. Second, readers don't care what the writer thinks and take the emphasis as a sarcastic insult.

6. In a running quote that spans more than one paragraph, omit quotation marks at the end of the paragraph, but use them to start the next.

> The mayor announced that, "Although budget problems will restrict street improvements, all our main objectives will be met.
> "Only some of the city's railroad crossings will have to wait for new surfacing."

However, partial quotations that end a paragraph must be enclosed in marks, even if the quotation is continued in the next paragraph.

> Then the mayor indicated his wish to "see this fiscal situation through to the end."
> "No state intervention will be necessary," he said.

7. Titles should be enclosed in quotation marks, except for names of magazines, newspapers, the Bible, reference books and musical scores that have numbers instead of names.

> "Gone With the Wind"
>
> The Chicago Tribune
>
> Britannica Atlas
>
> Symphony No. 3

8. Quotation marks usually enclose nicknames: William "Slam Dunk" Olson.

Hyphens

The hyphen should bring words together to work as a unit. Writers also insert it where it will avoid confusion.

1. Use the hyphen to unite compound modifiers before a noun unless the first modifier is *very* or an adverb ending in *-ly*.

> The story involved a seven-gable house.
>
> She brought a 3-year-old girl.
>
> It was a very involved relationship.
>
> He witnessed a slowly developing storm.

Distinguish between those instances when a set of words modifies another word, and when the words modify nothing.

> He said the steak was well-done.
>
> "Well done," she said.

2. Some prefixes and suffixes require hyphens, but unless the words are familiar ones it's best to check the dictionary. Hyphenate if the prefix joins with a capitalized word. If the prefix ends in a vowel and the next word starts with a vowel use a hyphen to avoid an awkward doubling of vowels.

> He developed an intra-axial drive shaft.

Exceptions are *cooperate* and *coordinate*.

3. Use hyphens in scores, votes, odds or ratios in constructions omitting the preposition.

The score was 21-19 at halftime.

The bookie gave 4-3 odds at kickoff.

The roof had a 3-12 pitch.

4. Use hyphens in compounds that are interrupted.

He painted his house and barn in four- and eight-year intervals, respectively.

That's called a *suspensive* hyphen.

Apostrophes

The following rules describe how to use apostrophes.

1. An apostrophe shows possession in nouns. Check the discussion of possessives on page 25.

2. An apostrophe indicates omissions in figures and omitted letters in contractions.

aren't, can't, bottled in '88, this 'n' that

3. An apostrophe makes a plural of a single letter.

Grades included 14 B's. We learned our three R's.

4. An apostrophe with a pronoun makes a contraction.

he's (he is), who's (who is)

But note that he's does not mean *he has,* and that he'd means *he would,* not *he had.* For clarity, it can't mean both.

5. An apostrophe can make possessives of indefinite pronouns: one's, another's, nobody's, anybody's, everybody's, somebody's.

Parentheses

The general rule for journalists is to use parentheses sparingly. In most cases they appear as obstacles to comprehension and rapid reading. Sometimes a newswriter will find them useful in setting off

1. Material in a direct quotation to explain words or phrases not clear from context

> The governor took a back road (Route 9) to the ranch.

2. Incidental or non-essential information

> Few people knew his age. (He told his aunt he was 45.)

If the added material isn't a complete sentence or depends on its sentence for meaning, place the period outside the parentheses.

> He received a limited weather report (no radar scan).

If the parenthetical material can stand alone as a complete sentence, place the period inside the parentheses.

> Travelers reported that most of the snow had melted on main highways. (Patrolmen left the garage without chains on their tires.)

Ellipses

An ellipsis, created with three spaced periods, indicates that something has been left out of a quotation, text or document. Never use an ellipsis, even for condensation, when it leaves a reader confused about the meaning. Always use an ellipsis if the material left out isn't known or available. Arbitrarily omitting an ellipsis in a quotation is the same as altering the quotation. If a speaker being quoted halts and abandons an important statement in mid-sentence, a writer should insert an ellipsis to indicate it. Otherwise, the speaker can appear to be an imbecile.

An ellipsis that comes after a complete sentence should follow the regular punctuation and a standard space. If an ellipsis comes at the end of one paragraph, one should appear at the beginning of the next.

Diagonals

The only useful purpose for a *diagonal* in newswriting is to indicate fractions of numbers beyond ½ and ¼, which appear on most keyboards: 3/4, 5/12, etc. Technically, the diagonal is a *virgule*. It's also called a *slash*.

Using a diagonal to indicate a choice (either/or, his/hers, and/or) invites confusion. It's better to find a substitute or to separate the two with *or*.

2

Common Language Blunders

7

Errors in Agreement

There was a writer named Dow,
Who was careless, we will allow.
To put it essentially,
He did things presently
When he should have done them now.

THE OBJECTIVE HERE is to show the more common blunders in journalistic writing and to present guidelines for achieving clarity and sense.

Person and Number

Subject and verb must agree, both in person and number.
Probably no other rule falls battered and broken so often as this one. It sounds simple enough, but it's tricky in several ways, and those tricky places are worth studying.
In most simple sentences it's easy to make a subject and verb agree in number.

A singular subject needs a singular verb.

John *is* alone.

A plural subject needs a plural verb.

John and Mary *are* alone.

The Johnsons *are* alone.

A first person subject requires a verb in first person.

I *am* late.

A second person subject needs a verb in second person.

You *are* late.

A third person subject needs a verb in third person.

He *is* late.

Problems show up when it's not clear which word or phrase forms the subject, or whether the subject is singular or plural.

When identifying the subject of a sentence remember that no matter how many phrases clutter the sentence between subject and verb, they shouldn't affect the number of the verb.

The reason for his visits *was* to gain her affection.

All the squad's officers, including the sergeant, *are* to be punished.

One of the excuses he gave his superiors *was* that his partner had abandoned him.

Whenever a phrase or clause forms the sentence's subject, consider the entire segment singular.

Planning for a restaurant's meals *takes* considerable time.

"Whatever the law allows" *means* taking some chances.

Subjects usually show up before the verbs in sentences, but they can follow the verb, causing doubts about whether the verb should be singular or plural. The writer often can transpose the sentence mentally and easily determine the proper number of the verb.

Directing traffic amid the crowd of police officers *was* Lieutenant Woods. (Lieutenant Woods is the subject, so it needs the singular verb.)

A compound subject is plural, so it requires a plural verb even when it follows the verb. This can be so confusing that it almost always requires transposing the sentence mentally when the subject follows the verb.

Trying to run the robber down *were* a homeowner and the neighborhood watchman.

Now, how can one determine the number of a sentence's subject, especially if it appears to have more than one? If the two are joined by *and* they usually need a plural verb.

The Police and Fire Divisions *are* under the Department of Public Safety.

Writing and reading *are* essentials for any aspiring journalist.

Sanding the wood and staining it *are* final steps for the woodworker.

But sometimes words that appear to form a compound subject take a singular verb because the writer must consider them a single unit. They may, for example, form a company name, involving several people or units.

Johnson & Sons *is* a local plumbing company.

Ham and eggs *is* his favorite breakfast.

Also, if the compound subject is preceded by *each* or *every* it is singular and needs a singular verb.

Each report and recommendation *is* acted upon.

Every salesman and shipper *has* a new order book.

Some words, such as *couple, family, group, minority, percent, people* and *personnel,* when used as subjects of sentences, can be either singular or plural and can take verbs to match. A writer usually can determine the number of a noun by deciding how the word is used in the sentence. If the word produces a feeling of a unit, use a singular verb.

The family *is* leaving tonight on an auto trip.

The young couple *was* lost in the big hotel.

The majority *is* able to set the schedule.

If parts of the noun can be separated into individuals or units, it needs a plural verb.

A group of lieutenants and sergeants *were* gathering in the square.

Another group of words, ending in *-ics (athletics, economics, politics, statistics,* etc.), also can take singular or plural verbs, depending on their use. The rule, again, is to determine by the word's use whether it collects into one, or separates into two or more.

> Politics *is* a demanding subject.

> The politics of both parties *call* for guts and glory.

Some pronouns (*another, each, either, neither* and *one*) are always singular. Also singular are all compound pronouns made with *any, every, no* and *some*. For example: nobody, anything, something, everyone.

> Nothing *is* so grand as a winter's day.

> Everybody who fills out the form *is* admitted.

> Neither he nor I *is* ready to admit failure.

> One of us *sends* the wrong message.

Some pronouns (*both, few, many, others* and *several*) are always plural.

> Few *are* expected to vote in the primary election, but many *are* expected in the fall.

The pronouns *all, any, more, most, none* and *some* are either plural or singular, depending on the noun they refer to.

> Most of the grain *is* spoiled. (Grain can't easily be counted, so it is singular, requiring a singular verb.)

> Most of the bushels *were* loaded. (Bushels is plural, requiring a plural verb.)

> Of all the kittens in the basket, none *was* white. (None here means "no kitten," requiring a singular verb.

About This and That

The demonstrative pronouns *this* and *that* are singular. *These* and *those* are plural. Too often the plural form gets paired improperly with a singular noun. Which choices would a journalist make from the following sentences?

> *These kind* of stories are hard to write.

> *These kinds* of stories are hard to write.

> *This kind* of story is hard to write.

Answer: Choose number two or three, in which the *number* of the pronoun agrees with that of its noun.

Money, Quantity and Time

Use a singular verb if it's a total amount.

> One hundred dollars *is* a small price today for a plumbing bill.

But use a plural verb when referring to individual parts.

> Three dollar bills *were* left on the dinner table.

Fractions

Choose the number of the verb from the number of the noun that follows the fraction.

> Half of the onions *were* planted.

> One-fourth of the ground *was* covered.

Either/or, Neither/nor

Make the verb singular when parts connected by either/or

or neither/nor are singular.

> Neither the Army nor the Navy *has* his records.

But if the connected parts are plural, make the verb plural.

> Either apples or oranges *make* a refreshing dessert.

If one connected part is singular and one is plural, follow the number of the part just before the verb.

> Either berries or an orange *is* easy to pack in a lunch.

Pronoun and Subject Agreement

It's just as important to make pronouns and subject antecedents agree in number as it is to make verbs and subjects agree.

> The City Council has passed *its* (not *their*) first budget.

> City workers are expected to turn in *their* expense records.

> Each police officer is asked to total *his* or *her* (not *their*) mileage account.

NOTE: The words *his or her* may seem awkward, but substituting the plural pronoun *their* in reference to a singular subject is far worse, even in the interest of fairness between the sexes. The best solution is to make everything plural.

> All police officers are asked to total *their* mileage accounts.

Other Pronoun Problems

Although it's elementary, it amazes editors every day to be reminded that some journalists don't remember that *which* normally refers to things, *who* refers to persons, and *that* can refer to either persons or things, preferably things.

When deciding whether to introduce a clause with *that* or *which,* it helps to apply a little test: If the clause can be omitted without leaving the noun it modifies incomplete or changing the meaning of the entire statement, or if the clause could be contained in parentheses, use *which.* Otherwise, use *that.*

More About That

Although brevity lies at the heart of news writing, it has always been a gamble to tell young journalists to remove unnecessary words. The word *that* seems to fall victim to this purge more than any other. Indeed, at times it should, but at other times removing it changes the sense of the sentence.

> He revealed *that* a photo had been taken of the scene.

The same sentence without *that* makes it appear that the word *photo* is the direct object of *revealed.* Without *that* the sentence takes readers down a side street and leaves them to find their way back unaided.

A sentence especially needs *that* when a time element comes between the verb and the clause. Otherwise a sentence suffers from this sort of awkwardness.

> The police chief announced Tuesday (*that*) officers should try to avoid high-speed chases. (Who are the Tuesday officers?)

Appearance of some words should invite the use of *that* in introducing a clause: *advocate, assert, contend, declare, estimate, make clear, point out, propose, state.*

Another easy clue: Use *that* before a direct quotation. Notice how its removal would tangle the meaning:

> The mayor told the council *that* to "involve building regulations in such a way would cause havoc among contractors."

Wrong Case of Pronouns

It isn't difficult to determine whether a pronoun is being used to indicate possession or as a subject, object, indirect object, etc., in relation to other words in a sentence. Still, many writers pick the wrong case. Here we'll treat only the most common errors.

> A group of *us* (not we) students visited City Hall. (Object of the preposition *of.*)

> *Whom* (not who) did she marry? (Object of the verb *did marry.*)

> This was between *me* and *her* (not I and she). (Object of the preposition *between.*)

> *Who* (not whom) gives this woman to this man? (*Who* is the subject, so must be in the *nominative* case.)

When a linking verb connects a pronoun to its antecedent subject, it must take the *nominative* case.

> It is *I* (not me).

> The new girl was *she* (not her).

When a pronoun is an *appositive* (beside another), it should appear in the same case as its partner.

> He asked *us* three—Jim, Mary and *me* (not I).

> *We* three—Jim, Mary and *I* (not me)—are invited.

Double Troubles

It's a common error to substitute the compound personal pronoun *myself* for I or me, maybe because the simple pronouns sound egotistical, or maybe because the writer has given up trying. Writers who wouldn't think of writing "He gave it to *myself*," will commit the blunder when the object of the preposition is doubled.

> He gave it to John and *myself*.

Similarly, those who would always write, "A cousin of *hers*," and never "A cousin of *her*," will often fall into a trap when the object is doubled. They will write, "A cousin of *her* and *me*," rather than the proper "A cousin of *hers* and *mine*." That's called a *double possessive*.

8

Modification, Construction Faults

There was a writer named Neeley,
Whose participles flew too freely.
They dangled, he knew,
But that's how they grew.
His meaning got lost in the melee.

Misplaced Modification

Too Far Away

Modifiers usually must stand close to the word or words they modify or get lost in the crowd, losing their meaning and creating confusion. Everybody is familiar with the problem of the misplaced adjective.

Police reported finding a *black* woman's bag.

Queen Victoria was the *longest* ruler in English history.

One modifier, the word *only*, provides a good example. It can appear almost anywhere in a sentence and produce a different meaning in each position. Writers probably misplace it more than any other word in our language. Here is a simple sentence to illustrate how it can trip a careless writer.

I saw him on the beach yesterday.

Now, in sequence, place the word *only* before each word in the sentence, reading the sentence each time to illustrate how the meaning changes. Writers and editors should stop each time they encounter that word and determine its proper position before moving on.

Here's another misplaced modifier.

> He *almost* read all of the assignment.

That seems correct grammatically, but if the writer means that the subject read *almost all* of the assignment, that's the way to write it. In placing modifiers writers must always ask their sources, and themselves, what they mean to say.

> **Wrong:** He said he wasn't sure John was a *safe* person to leave in the community.
>
> **Right:** He said he wasn't sure it was *safe* to leave John in the community.

> **Wrong:** Police said they stopped a *suspicious* vehicle.
>
> **Right:** Police said they became *suspicious* and stopped a vehicle.

> **Wrong:** Coach Adams couldn't believe that his Tigers had beaten three *straight* ranked teams at home.
>
> **Right:** Coach Adams couldn't believe that his Tigers had beaten ranked teams at home three games *straight*.

Misplacing modifiers can cause embarrassment in addition to strangling communication.

> The fire fighter arranged to discuss the dangers of leaking gas *from the podium*.

> The woodworker decided to stain the table for the customer *wearing only a gauze mask*.

Police officers pulled the woman *inside* out.

The deacon was convicted of raping his cousin *in District Court.*

The robber shot her *through the window.*

The intruder was knifed *in the process.*

Modifying the wrong word can cause a writer to choose the wrong modifier. Substituting *adjectives* in places that need *adverbs,* for example, has become epidemic. Remember that adverbs modify verbs, adjectives or other adverbs. Adjectives modify nouns, pronouns or other adjectives. Writers must ask themselves constantly which words require modification.

Wrong: He suffered an *apparent* heart attack. (Adjective *apparent* modifies heart attack.)

Right: *Apparently* he suffered a heart attack. (Adverb *apparently* modifies suffered.)

Wrong: The Redskin defense is playing *outstanding.*

Right: The Redskin defense is playing *outstandingly.*
or
The Redskin defense is *outstanding.*

It can get worse.

Wrong: The city received six inches of *official* snow. (Only city officials shower us with official snow.)

Right: *Officially* the city received six inches of snow. (The adverb *officially* modifies the verb received.)

Danglers

A writer can get into trouble easily by throwing in a modifying phrase haphazardly, away from the word it modifies, or forgetting to make the subject of the main clause clear. These examples all came from published newspaper stories.

> *When lathered in motor oil* you can see the leak from the head gasket. (Here it improperly modifies *you*, not *head gasket*.)

> *After sitting on the shuttle's robot arm an extra day,* ground controllers succeeded in freeing the satellite for its mission. (Here the phrase improperly modifies *ground controllers* instead of *satellite*.)

> *When only three* her father moved out. (Here it improperly modifies *father*.)

> *Hanging broken and rusty* he found time to fix the old gate. (Here it improperly modifies *he*.)

> *Once buttered,* she added a generous amount of sugar. (Here it improperly modifies *she*.)

Stacking Modifiers

In awkward attempts at description some writers persist in stringing modifiers together. Adjectives and adverbs provide questionable description, and piling them on doesn't do much but confuse readers.

> *Bleak, damp, cloudy, cold* weather had set in.

Instead, it's usually best to forgo the modifiers and create an overall *effect* upon those experiencing the event, always making certain it's true.

> The weather *depressed* everyone.

Titles, another form of modifier, can be stacked in ungainly clusters also, and can obstruct the sense of a sentence.

Next the committee took its case to *Deputy Director of Services for Naval Dependents* Capt. George Hocking.

Writers usually can incorporate such titles into a statement describing what the titled person *does*.

Next the committee took its case to Capt. George Hocking, who *helps arrange service and assistance for naval dependents.*

Lack of Parallel Construction

Use parallel terms to express parallel thoughts in sequence. It strengthens writing by improving the flow. A writer who starts a sequence using one verbal form, gerunds, for instance, should complete the sequence with gerunds and not switch to an infinitive form. Similarly, a sequence started with one prepositional phrase should stay with that preposition for the rest of the sequence.

Wrong: Fishing is more fun than to hunt.
Right: Fishing is more fun than hunting.

Wrong: They came on foot, by car and horseback.
Right: They came by foot, by car and by horseback.

Trying to express *ranges* can cause problems in parallelism. *Between* pairs with *and*. *From* pairs with *to*.

Visitors arrived *between* 6 *and* 10 p.m.

He wrote *from* May *to* July.

Avoid placing individual words to make them parallel with clauses.

Wrong: She is careful about what she eats, drinks and the
medicine she takes.

Right: She is careful about the medicine she takes and
what she eats and drinks.

Even actions and lists of things should follow parallel forms
for clarity.

Sentence Fragments

We've all spoken in sentences since early childhood, but the
incomplete sentence or sentence fragment appears more often
than many other language faults, even in newsrooms. If it lacks
a subject or verb or if the writer brings it to a full stop without
expressing a complete thought, it's a fragment and needs rescue.
It leaves a reader waiting expectantly for the missing part.

More often than not the writer of an incomplete sentence
changed course somewhere in mid-thought and didn't complete
the original idea. News editors encounter swarms of complex
dependent clauses that somehow have broken loose from their
main clauses.

Despite the fact that he had paid his fees and bought his
tickets

Under the old pine trees about the time the sun turned
orange on the horizon

Fragments can serve a writer well when used for a purpose.
Feature stories, speeches and advertising copy allow relaxed rules,
but in most cases it's best to read one's own words carefully
and apply the test of the complete thought.

Run-on Sentences

Clauses need periods after the complete thought, or conjunctions to join them to other complete thoughts. Too many writers carelessly toss in a comma and rush ahead to the next idea, hoping that readers will understand. Sometimes called a "comma splice," this error creates incoherence and easily throws the reader into confusion.

> Three airplanes tore loose from their moorings, a fire crew attacked the blaze in one of the hangars.

> Storm clouds rolled toward the unsuspecting villagers, rain started pelting dry cornfields.

Substituting periods for the commas will correct many of these run-ons. Conjunctions can connect the clauses if they are of equal weight.

> Farmers registered for their set-aside allowances, but few thought the checks would compensate for their reduced production.

False Conjunctions

The word *with*, a preposition, has a multitude of uses and even meanings. It can't reasonably play the role of conjunction, however, as some writers ask it to do. A writer can refer to a man *with* brown hair, but not this way.

> He has brown eyes *with* brown hair.

The preposition in that sentence tries to take the place of *and*. The conjunction would add clarity, avoiding the impression that the eyes have brown hair.

Here's another example.

> The forecast is cloudy skies *with* temperatures in the 60s.

The temperatures don't belong to or go with the skies. Again, *and* will connect parts of the forecast of equal rank.

Non Sequiturs

Non sequiturs are irrelevancies introduced into sentences by writers who forget or ignore where they're going. Phrases and clauses linked together physically ought to have some connection in meaning. But non sequiturs wound the normal logic of association and result in part of a sentence taking a detour. Such sentences appear to have been written by committees and often arise from efforts to mesh background material into current developments.

> Mrs. Johnson, *a woman who loved to grow roses for national shows,* was beaten fatally outside her hotel in downtown Portland.

> Gen. Wayne, *who often rode his horse in local parades,* ordered his artillery to open fire.

> *Born in North Dakota,* the author could not accept non sequiturs.

Problems With Verbs

Too Many Verbs

It's easy to fall into a habit of tossing extra clauses into sentences. It's how we speak, unfortunately, and if we write that way we fuzz over our meaning and add verbiage. Technically, it's called *over-predication,* because it introduces unnecessary verb forms. Any clause or sentence that begins with the words *there is, there are, there has been,* etc., provides a useful danger sign.

Wrong:	*There is* a peaceful town named Elmwood *that* offers visitors its hospitality.
Right:	The peaceful town of Elmwood offers visitors its hospitality.

Wrong:	*What* the salesperson tries to *do is* fill the order book before the month ends.
Right:	The salesperson tries to fill the order book before the month ends.

Wrong:	He had to decide what *it is* he wants to do.
Right:	He had to decide what he wants to do.

Here's an example of *super* over-predication.

It is the case that there are some people *who* never eat breakfast.

Interrupted Compound Verbs

It isn't the world's worst sin to drop an adverb into the middle of a compound verb or to split away the *to* in the infinitive form. All good writers have broken their verbs for good purpose. Sometimes it's less awkward to do so, or the result falls more gently on the ear. Even so, it is usually best not to interrupt compound verbs. This caution is directed at those who insist on divorcing all verbs from their auxiliaries.

Split:	He began *to slowly retrace* his steps to learn where he had lost the trail.
Better:	Slowly he began *to retrace* his steps to learn where he had lost the trail.

Split: Sometimes she *would tentatively start* to the telephone, then change her mind.
Better: Sometimes she *would start* tentatively to the telephone, then change her mind.

Split: The bus *had gradually disappeared* beyond the trees.
Better: The bus *had disappeared* gradually beyond the trees.

Keep Verb Tenses Simple

Writers ought to keep verb tenses simple whenever
possible. Some seem incapable of using a simple present or past
tense. Instead, they weigh their readers down with participle
forms, which become necessary only when one must provide a
sense of continuing action.

> **Weighed down:** He *was working* nine hours every day.
> **Better:** He *worked* nine hours every day.

> **Weighed down:** She *is riding* the bus to work.
> **Better:** She *rides* the bus to work.

Wrong Verb Form

It's far too common to see the wrong forms or spellings for
verbs in *past* or *past participle* tense. Some irregular verbs cause
special problems because writers aren't sure of their ground.
Verbs listed here in present, past and past participle forms are
those most commonly abused.

Present	Past	Past Participle
awake	awoke	awaked (not awakened)
bear	bore	borne
bid (as an offer)	bid	bid
bid (to order)	bade	bidden
bring	brought	brought
broadcast	broadcast	broadcast
burst	burst	burst

Present	Past	Past Participle
choose	chose	chosen
cling	clung	clung
dive	dived (not dove)	dived
drag	dragged (not drug)	dragged
drink	drank	drunk
drown	drowned	drowned
flow	flowed	flowed
fly (as a bird)	flew	flown
forbid	forbade	forbidden
forsake	forsook	forsaken
get	got	got or gotten
hang (execute)	hanged	hanged
hang (suspend)	hung	hung
kneel	knelt or kneeled	knelt or kneeled
lay (to place)	laid	laid
lead	led	led
lie (recline)	lay	lain
plead	pleaded (not pled)	pleaded
prove	proved (not proven)	proved (not proven)
rise	rose	risen
set (to place)	set	set
shake	shook	shaken
shine	shone	shone
show	showed (or shown)	showed (or shown)
sit (in chair)	sat	sat
slay	slew	slain
sneak	sneaked (not snuck)	sneaked
steal	stole	stolen
strive	strove	striven
swim	swam	swum
tread	trod	trod (or trodden)
wake	woke (or waked)	waked
weave	wove	woven

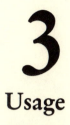

3
Usage

9

What's Right, Wrong

There was a writer named Dresser,
Whose words dismayed his professor.
We asked, "Was it usage?"
He said, "'Twas abusage.
Dresser is best as a guesser."

Searching for Rules

Correct usage of words separates good writers and editors from the rest. The rub comes in defining "correct" usage because of the nature of the language and how it grows. We even expect experts to disagree, but that shouldn't excuse us from searching for good rules. Whose models a writer follows isn't as important as respecting an authority on usage or checking dictionaries for definitions. Improper usage of words follows more often from failure to inquire than from a disagreement among experts.

Substantial amounts of reading and writing probably overcome most of our faults in usage, just as they help remedy grammar and other language weaknesses. Reading the work of reputable writers of all periods helps news people to recognize improper usage, an ability that comes from developing an "ear" for correctness. This ear, or feel for clarity and acceptability can provide a reliable authority even while the uses of words are undergoing change.

Using a word correctly makes our writing as enlightened as our intentions. Incorrect usage tears a hole in the fabric of communication. It diminishes the clarity and thereby the value of the word improperly used. Misused regularly, a word loses some of its meaning because readers become less certain of its definition. Many English words have fallen from use, and indeed should be discarded, because misuse has destroyed them. Such words lie as casualties when we allow illiteracy and carelessness to drive language's evolution.

Grammar, punctuation and spelling change slowly, so the commonly heard expression that English is always changing can be narrowed largely to the uses of words. When we refer to a "new expression," we don't usually mean new words. We refer to old words used with new meanings. They may appear in new combinations or with new appendages. In using the new expression, some people, and eventually a whole group, change the way they refer to a thing or an act. Those who start the expression may not be aware of their new usage, but it seems to fill a need for them.

Whether the new expression catches on depends mostly on its usefulness, whether it provides meaning that isn't already available in other clear, simple English words. Expressions and usages that become generally accepted contribute to building the world's most expressive language. Those that fail to gain or hold acceptance gradually disappear.

Journalists hold a vital position in policing the growth of their language. If that statement seems a gross presumption, consider the size of a journalist's everyday audience and the influence exerted in choosing precise words for every line of type. If a new expression doesn't add clarity, simplicity and richness of meaning already available in other words, it's weak and very likely won't gain acceptance. Some terms and expressions stay around for a while as fads and then disappear. Even an added shade of sense can be valuable, however, so nobody should reject new expressions simply because they are new or because old expressions come close.

New expressions, even words whose meanings have changed, must achieve general acceptance before being used in news stories, because newspapers circulate to relatively general audiences. A new term or expression circulating on university campuses, for example, can leave a broader readership confused and uninformed. An expression, no matter how accepted it may be on a city's streets, probably won't mean much outside those areas. In this sense they are like the jargon of specialists: They have not entered the general marketplace and must be translated.

Again, to make these judgments journalists must read and circulate beyond the boundaries of their beats, their families and their own interests. They become valuable communicators of ideas and information only if they can apply tests of word acceptability and usage dozens of times a day. It's called intervening in the interest of the reader.

Words are a journalist's most important tools, just as cutting and shaving devices are a cabinetmaker's most important tools. Neither the woodworker nor the writer who abuses or misuses tools can expect to remain effective and stay in business for long. The instruments won't continue to do their work. Anyone who takes language responsibility seriously has compiled long lists of words or phrases carelessly abused or misused. If nothing else, such lists stand as proof that those who compile them care about words.

Much word misuse originates in careless speech, which precedes the pen in language evolution. Those who put words on paper control and guard the floodgates of change. Each word or phrase heedlessly spoken easily grows into a language fault, because in a modern society fewer people than ever put their words in writing. Even letters to relatives and memos within the office have fallen victim to the telephone and the intercom. Those who may be pressed by events to transfer their spoken words to paper are reminded how the writing discipline forces more thought, and how it demands more attention to meaning and clarity.

Error by Association

We can understand common usage problems better if we group examples by form. Some words can change or suffer from confusion and abuse because of their association with other words by spelling or some other likeness. To confuse such words bends their meaning, and that's as perilous for a journalist as it is for a woodworker to bend the edge of a cutting blade. Here's a list of the most commonly confused words.

Adapt: To adjust.
Adopt: To approve or accept.

Adverse: Unfavorable. Things, such as weather, are *adverse.*
Averse: Opposed. People can be *averse* to ideas, for example.

Affect: A verb. To influence.
Effect: Usually a noun. The result. But it also can be a verb meaning to bring about, as in to *effect* a change.

Affluence: Abundance.
Effluence: A flowing out, or a thing that flows out.
Effluents: The outflow of a sewer.

Aid: Help.
Aide: A helper, assistant.

Allude: To mention, refer to.
Elude: To avoid, escape or evade.

Altogether: Wholly, completely. Everything being considered. For example: He ate five fish *altogether.*
All together: Everything at one time or place. For example: "We were *all together* in the yard."

Alumna: Singular. A woman who has attended a school.
Alumnus: Singular. A man who has attended a school.
Alumnae: Plural. Women who have attended a school.
Alumni: Plural. Men and women who have attended a school.

Amoral: Not to be judged by moral standards.
Immoral: Opposed to a moral code.

Anecdote: An amusing story.
Antidote: A remedy to counteract a poison.

Appose: To position side by side.
Oppose: To be or set against.

Assay: To test.
Essay: A written composition in prose. To try.

Avert: To prevent, ward off.
Avoid: To shun, stay clear of.

Baited: Lured by an attraction, as in *baiting* a hook.
Bated: A form of *abated.* Held, as in *bated* breath.

Baloney: A slang word for nonsense.
Bologna: A processed lunch meat.

Bazaar: A marketplace.
Bizarre: Odd, unusual.

Beside: At the side.
Besides: In addition to.

Biannual: Twice a year.
Biennial: Every two years.

Block: Many definitions. Nouns involving mass, verbs
            involving to impede.
Bloc: A grouping or coalition of persons with common
          purpose.

Born: Given birth.
Borne: To have given birth, to have endured, to have
            carried, as with a load.

Bouillon: A broth.
Bullion: Gold or silver in ingots.

Brahman: A breed of cattle. A Hindu caste.
Brahmin: An aristocrat.

Breach: A violation. An opening or tear.
Breech: Rear, back or bottom.

Britain: The country.
Briton: A native or inhabitant of the country.

Burro: An ass.
Burrow: A hole, usually dug by an animal. To dig.

Bus: A mass transit vehicle. Spelled *buses* as plural and *buses* and *busing* as verb.
Buss: A kiss.

Cannon: A large gun.
Canon: A church law.

Canvas: A heavy cloth for tents, awnings.
Canvass: To solicit for votes, opinions, orders.

Capital: The city, seat of government.
Capitol: The building, seat of government.

Carat: A unit for weighing diamonds, other gems.
Caret: An editing mark to indicate an insertion.
Karat: A measure of the purity of gold.

Careen: To sway, as in a ship.
Career: To move at full speed.
Carom: To rebound, as a billiard ball.

Celebrant: A participant or leader of a religious service.
Celebrator: One who participates in a non-religious celebration.

Censor: To judge, or one who previews and judges before public release of material.
Censure: An official reprimand.

Childish: A derogatory word applied to adults.
Childlike: A favorable word applied to adults.

Chord: Notes that harmonize.
Cord: String or rope. Quantity of firewood. Nerve system in spine.

Cite: To quote others in support.
Site: A place.

Classic: A thing long recognized as a model of superior quality.
Classical: Reference to a specific historical time: ancient Greece and Rome.

Climactic: About a climax.
Climatic: About weather.

Complement: To complete or bring to perfection. That which completes, etc.
Compliment: Praise, or to praise.

Compose: The parts *compose*, or make up, the whole.
Comprise: The whole is *comprised*, or made up, of the parts.

Consul: Diplomat.
Council: A deliberating or legislative body. Group of advisers.
Counsel: An adviser. Advice. To advise.

Continual: Repeated.
Continuous: Uninterrupted.

Corespondent: Another who is accused with a defendant.

Co-respondent: In a divorce case, a person charged with adultery with another person from whom the divorce is sought.

Correspondent: One who communicates by writing. Anything that matches.

Criteria: Plural. Standards, rules or tests.

Criterion: Singular. Standard, rule or test.

Crochet: A variation of knitting.

Crotchet: A peculiar whim or stubborn notion.

Deadly: Anything that brings death.

Deathly: Anything that resembles death.

Defuse: To stop, as in removing a fuse.

Diffuse: To scatter.

Deprecate: To feel or express disapproval.

Depreciate: To lessen in value or price. Also, to belittle or disparage.

Disassemble: To take apart.

Dissemble: To conceal under a false appearance.

Discreet: Careful. Prudent.

Discrete: Separate and distinct.

Distinctive: Noticeably different and recognizable.

Distinguished: Eminent or outstanding.

Drier: Not so moist.

Dryer: A machine for drying.

Dual: Having two parts. Two-fold.
Duel: A fight, sometimes formal, between two persons.

Economic: Refers to finances.
Economical: Saving, thrifty.

Egotism: Referring constantly to oneself.
Egoism: Considering other things only as they bear upon
oneself.

Elder: A comparison in the relative ages of persons.
Older: A comparison of the ages of any old things.

Elegy: A sad poem or song.
Eulogy: Oration at a funeral.

Elicit: To get from or draw out.
Illicit: Not allowed by rule, law.

Emigrate: To move away, depart one area or country to
go to another.
Immigrate: To come into a new country from another.

Eminent: Prominent.
Imminent: Soon to happen.

Enormous: Huge, vast, immense.
Enormity: Great wickedness. An outrageous act.

Ensure: To make an outcome certain.
Insure: To provide insurance for things or lives.

Envelop: To surround.
Envelope: Container for a letter.

Evoke: To call forth, summon.
Invoke: To ask solemnly for, implore, entreat.

Exalt: To praise. To raise in rank.
Exult: To rejoice, be jubilant.

Expatriate: One who has withdrawn or been driven from his native land. To drive one from his native land.
Ex-patriot: One who has lost loyalty and love for a native land.

Farther: More distant in physical terms.
Further: More or additional time or degree.

Flail: A whip, scourge. To whip or beat.
Flay: To strip off the skin or hide as by beating.

Flair: An aptitude or talent.
Flare: A dazzling light.

Flounder: A fish. To struggle helplessly.
Founder: To sink.

Flaunt: To display ostentatiously.
Flout: To show disdain for. To mock or scoff.

Flu: Influenza.
Flue: A duct to carry smoke.

Forbear: To refrain from or cease.
Forebear: An ancestor.

Forbidding: Difficult.
Foreboding: Ominous. A prediction or portent.

Foregoing: Going before.
Forgoing: To go without.

Fortuitous: Accidental. Happening by chance.
Fortunate: Lucky.

Fullness: The quality or state of being full.
Fulsome: Disgusting or offensive, especially because of excess or insincerity.

Gantlet: Refers to a punishment in which a person passes between two files of individuals to be beaten.
Gauntlet: A glove, often referred to as being thrown to the ground as a challenge.
Gamut: A scale of musical notes.

Gibe: To taunt.
Jibe: To change course. To be in accord.

Gorilla: An ape.
Guerrilla: An irregular soldier.

Hail: To signal or salute. Precipitated ice.
Hale: To haul or take, as to jail. In good health.

Hangar: A shelter for aircraft.
Hanger: A device on which something hangs.

Hapless: Unfortunate. Luckless.
Hopeless: Without hope.

Healthy: Good physical condition. People, plants, animals, can be *healthy* or unhealthy. Sports writers have bent the word to mean *ready to play*.

Healthful: Anything conducive to good physical condition. Food is *healthful* or unhealthful.

Heroin: A drug.
Heroine: A female hero, but a form no longer used.

Historic: What has a place in history.
Historical: What refers or pertains to history.

Hoard: To store. A storehouse.
Horde: A crowd, pack, swarm.

Imply: The speaker or writer *implies*, meaning to hint or indicate meaning.
Infer: The listener or reader *infers*, which is to take meaning from the speaker's or writer's words.

Imposter: A person who levies a tax.
Impostor: One who pretends to be another.

Impracticable: Not feasible or capable of being carried out.
Impractical: Not valuable for use. Not practical.

Incredible: Unbelievable.
Incredulous: Skeptical.

Ingenious: Inventive.
Ingenuous: Honest, open, forthright.

Insoluble: What can't be dissolved.
Insolvable: What can't be solved.

Interment: Burial.
Internment: Detention as an enemy alien or soldier.

Interstate: Between states.
Intrastate: Within a state.

Its: Possessive for *it.*
It's: Contraction of *it is.*

Judicial: Reference to a judge or court.
Judicious: Sound in judgment.

Lay: To put or place.
Lie: To put oneself in reclining position. A state of being.
(The past tense of *lie* is *lay,* which adds to confusion.)

Leach: Separation of solids from liquid solutions by
percolation, as through soil.
Leech: To suck blood. A bloodsucker.

Lean: To stand diagonally, perhaps against something.
Lien: A legal right to sell the property of another in
settlement of a debt.

Lend: Verb. To give money or a thing that is to be repaid
or returned.
Loan: Noun. Money or a thing that is to be repaid or
returned to the giver.

Levee: Bank of a river.
Levy: A tax. To impose a tax.

Liable: Exposed to something unpleasant or disadvanta-
geous.
Likely: Probable or expected.

Livid: Black and blue or grayish blue, as with rage.
Vivid: Full of life, vigorous, lively, striking.

Loath: Reluctant. Takes the preposition *to*.
Loathe: Verb. To dislike.

Mantel: A shelf-like structure above a fireplace.
Mantle: A loose, sleeveless cape. An outer covering.

Marshall: A proper noun, as in John Marshall.
Marshal: To gather. Also used as a civil or military title.
Martial: Warlike. Relating to the military.

Masterful: Domineering, imperious.
Masterly: Expert, skillful.

Material: Anything used to make something.
Materiel: Supplies used by the military.

Media: Plural. Means, agencies of communication.
Medium: Singular. Agency of communication. Also, a
middle state or degree.

Minimize: To reduce to the least possible.
Minimum: The least possible.

Moral: Adjective: virtuous. Noun: a lesson.
Morale: Spirit or confidence.

Nauseated: The feeling of an upset stomach.
Nauseous: Describes whatever makes a stomach upset.

Noisy: Making or accompanied by noise.
Noisome: Injurious to health, noxious, stinking.

Notable: Worth taking notice
Notorious: Having a bad standing or reputation.

Official: Holding a position of authority. Coming from authority.
Officious: Obliging. Offering unwanted advice.

Ordinance: A law.
Ordnance: Weapons and ammunition.

Palate: Roof of the mouth.
Pallette: A small surface for mixing paints.
Pallet: A thin, hard bed. A cargo platform.

Parameter: In mathematics, a constant whose value varies with its application.
Perimeter: The outer boundary of an area.

Parlay: To increase.
Parley: To talk.

Pendant: Noun. An ornament worn around the neck.
Pendent: Adjective. Hanging.

Peremptory: Final, absolute, decisive.
Pre-emptory: Being pre-emptive, seizing before anyone else can.

Perquisite: A privilege.
Prerequisite: A requirement.

Persecute: To oppress.
Prosecute: To conduct legal proceedings against.

Perspective: A view, scene.
Prospective: Expected.

Populous: Adjective. Filled with people.
Populace: The masses of common people.

Pore: To study carefully.
Pour: To cause a liquid to flow.

Premier: First or prime minister. First in importance.
Premiere: A first performance of a play. Not a verb.

Prescribe: To set down as direction or order.
Proscribe: To outlaw, denounce, forbid.

Presumptive: Based on presumption.
Presumptuous: Too bold or forward.

Pretense: An unsupported claim of distinction or accomplishment.
Pretext: Excuse. A false reason put forth to hide the real one.

Principle: Noun. A guiding rule or basic truth.
Principal: Noun or adjective. The first, dominant or leading thing. Also a title.

Prodigy: Someone or something extraordinary.
Protégé: A person under the protection or care of another.

Prophecy: Noun. Prediction.
Prophesy: Verb. To predict.

Proved: Past tense of prove.
Proven: Tested as effective.

Qualitative: Does not refer to quality but to the kind or parts being examined.
Quantitative: Refers to the number of parts being examined.

Rack: Framework. Instrument of torture. To arrange. To torture.
Wrack: Ruin. Destruction. To wreck.
Wreak: To give vent to anger. To inflict.

Refute: To prove false or wrongful.
Dispute: To argue or oppose.

Relation: To denote a kinsman. "Not related to" or "no relation of," but never "no relation to."
Relative: Preferred reference to a kinsman.

Repulse: To drive back or beat back.
Repel: To cause distaste or dislike in.

Review: A scholarly or critical examination.
Revue: A light theatrical production.

Rout: A defeat resulting in confusion and retreat.
Route: A road, way or course traveled.

Sculptor: A creator of three-dimensional art.
Sculpture: Three-dimensional art.

Seasonable: Timely or correct for the season.
Seasonal: Associated with the seasons.

Sensual: Refers to gratification of the animal senses.
Sensuous: Refers to enjoyment of the pleasures of sensation.

Set: A verb that usually transfers action to an object, as in placing an object.
Sit: A verb usually requiring no object, as in "John *sits* in a chair."

Sewage: The material that passes through a *sewerage* system.
Sewerage: A system that includes sewers, that carries *sewage*.

Sleight: Skill, as in deceiving.
Slight: Adjective: meager. Verb: to neglect.

Sometime: A point of time, as in "sometime last week."
Some time: Written as two words when the meaning is a *long time*, a *short time* or an *indefinite time*: "Some time in the future."

Specious: Seeming to be sound without really being so. Used with abstract things. "The ideas are specious."
Spurious: Counterfeit. Used with concrete things. "The money was spurious."

Stanch: Verb. To stop or restrain, as in flow of blood.
Staunch: Adjective. Firm.

Stimulant: Anything that stimulates, as alcohol or drug.
Stimulus: A goad. Anything that rouses to action.

Straight: Not crooked.
Strait: A constriction or a narrow passage.

Suit: Clothing. A lawsuit. To please.
Suite: A set of furniture or rooms. Dance sets.

Superficial: Shallow. Near the surface.
Superfluous: More than necessary.

Suspect: To distrust, or believe another to be bad, wrong, harmful, questionable. One who is believed to be bad, wrong, harmful, questionable.
Expect: To look for as likely to occur.

Systematic: Following a plan.
Systemic: Affecting the entire system.

Tack: A course of action or policy.
Tact: Delicate sense of the right thing to say or do without offending.

Tempera: A process used in painting.
Tempura: A kind of cooking.

Their: Possessive for *they*.
They're: Contraction of *they are*.
There: At that place.

Thrash: To beat an opponent. To discuss for a settlement.
Thresh: To separate grain from straw.

Tort: Legal term for a wrongful act.
Torte: A rich cake.

Troop: A group of people or animals. Especially applied to military or police.

Troupe: A theatrical or performing group.

Turbid: Cloudy or muddled.

Turgid: Bombastic, inflated, grandiose.

Venal: Corruptible.

Venial: Minor or excusable.

Veracious: Truthful.

Voracious: Extremely hungry.

Vertex: The high point.

Vortex: A whirling body of water or air.

Waive: To pass, give up a chance.

Wave: To signal. To move to and fro, fluctuate.

Wangle: To obtain by manipulation.

Wrangle: To dispute or argue angrily and noisily.

Way: Used after *under* (two words) to indicate movement, as of a ship, program, etc.

Weigh: Used with *anchor* to indicate raising the device before a ship gets *under way*.

Whose: Possessive for *who*.

Who's: Contraction of *who is*.

Yoga: A discipline of the mind and body.

Yogi: One who follows the discipline of yoga.

10

Close Doesn't Count

There was a writer named Bender,
Who knew not sex from gender.
His readers, he'd shout,
Would figure it out,
But his stories came back to sender.

WRITERS CONFUSE many other words, some not even close in meaning, causing misuse of one or both. Some abuses appear so often they seem to feed on themselves, contributing to the feeling that bad language tends to drive out good language. Note that most definitions in this list cover only the usage in question.

After: Preposition. Later, next, next to in rank.
Following: Adjective. That follows.

It's confusing to make *following* a preposition: He arrived *following* the instructions. Use it in this sense: She gave the *following* orders: . . .

About: Nearly, approximately.
Approximately: Nearly, about.
Some: A certain one or ones not specified or known. Also a certain but not specified number, quantity or degree.

In the interest of simplicity and brevity why use the long and ungainly *approximately* when we have *about* about? And use either word only with imprecise figures, not "The court chose its panel from *about* 73 potential jurors." *Some* clearly can't replace either of the others, as in "*Some* 50 people arrived for the party."

Amateur: Not a professional.
Novice: A beginner.

Accident: A chance occurrence, good or bad, major or minor.
Mishap: An unfortunate occurrence, always minor.

Far too many people are killed these days in *mishaps.* Reserve the term for tripping over the bicycle or mangling a fender.

Aggravate: To make an existing condition worse.
Irritate: To cause inflammation or soreness.
Annoy: To vex or bother.

The culprits here are *aggravate* and *irritate,* often used incorrectly in place of *annoy.* One could *aggravate* an existing inflammation, but neither it nor *irritate* should be used in place of *annoy.*

Alibi: A term for a legal defense meaning that one was at another place when a crime occurred.
Excuse: A reason given when asking to be forgiven.

Excuse fills our requirements in most cases, the exception being the legal sense.

Allude: To mention in a casual way.
Refer: To direct attention to.

The contrast here is much the same as that between a glancing blow and a sock in the eye.

Among: Amidst more than two, but countable, persons or things.
Between: A separation or connection of two parts.
Amid or amidst: Contained within things not separable.

Generally speaking, nothing can happen *among* two people or things, or *between* more than two. When the parts aren't countable the correct word is *amid* or *amidst.*

Anxious: Desirous, but with some apprehension.
Eager: Desirous, but without apprehension.

Some students become *anxious* about their grades, but most are *eager* to learn.

Arbitrate: To hear evidence and judge before making an award.
Mediate: To act between two persons or sides and try to reach accord. Must be used with *between* or *among*.

Argument: Strictly speaking, it's a discussion or debate.
Quarrel: A dispute or disagreement, usually marked by anger and resentment.

The errant word here usually is *argument*, as in describing a dispute between neighbors. Use *quarrel* in such cases to be clear and to preserve the meaning of *argument*.

Balance: In bookkeeping, debits subtracted from credits.
Remainder: A small portion left over.

It's all too common to write *balance* for whatever *remains* in any division or transaction.

Because: Provides a reason or cause.
Since: Refers to a period of time.

This example illustrates the difference: "The years have passed quickly *since* the war *because* we have been busy starting our careers." Also, never write: The reason is *because* . . . (The reason is *that* it is redundant.)

Because of: By reason of. On account of.
Due to: Caused by. Owing to.

If a writer wishes to match cause to effect, *because of* is correct. If the question *why* can be answered, use *because of*. Use *due to* only with a linking verb in describing the condition of the subject: "The temperature drop was *due to* cloudiness."

Belly: A good nontechnical word for the body between chest and hips.

Abdomen: Scientific word for the body between chest and hips.

Stomach: Limited to one organ of the digestive system.

Too many writers don't have the *stomach* for *belly*.

Auditions: Test performances that are listened to.

Tryouts: Test performances that are watched.

Blatant: What calls attention, especially because of obtrusive sound.

Flagrant: Glaringly, notoriously, openly evil or scandalous.

Boat: A small open vessel. The exception is the submarine.

Ship: A seagoing vessel. It may carry a *boat*.

Journalists will ignore this distinction only if they wish to annoy their seagoing readers. Those who insist on going by *boat* should row their own.

Bring: To carry toward.

Take: To carry away.

As with the pairs, *imply* and *infer*, and *emigrate* and *immigrate*, the distinction between *bring* and *take* depends on the observer's position or role. Those who confuse such pairs don't know if they're coming or going.

Burglar: A specific kind of robber who breaks and enters in order to commit a felony.
Thief: One who steals secretly or stealthily.
Robber: One who steals by the use or threat of force.

Legal technicalities though they may be, these definitions draw useful lines for better understanding.

Cartridge: A complete unit or round of ammunition, including primer, propellant and projectile.
Bullet: Only the projectile of a round of ammunition.
Shell: An imprecise term regarding small arms ammunition, ambiguously applied to both cartridge and bullet.

One can't supply too much precision in describing crime and war, so avoid *shell* except when referring to large caliber ammunition. An *empty cartridge* refers to the brass container without propellant and projectile.

Citizen: One who takes part in the politics of a nation. One who holds legal citizenship.
Resident: One who lives in a designated area.

Too many *residents* never become *citizens*.

Client: One who uses a professional's services.
Customer: One who buys.

Collision: Two moving objects striking.
Crash: A moving object strikes an object, either moving or stationary.

Police reporters trying too hard not to place blame in reporting an accident have been known to write that a car was "in collision with" a light pole.

Compulsive: Obsessive.
Impulsive: Out of whim. Spontaneous.

Concert: An instrumental or vocal performance by two or more, not counting an accompanist.
Recital: A musical performance by a soloist, even one who appears with accompanist.

Concrete: Rock-hard construction material made from cement, gravel and water.
Cement: A powdered limestone product used in making concrete and mortar.

Connive: To conspire by cooperation in wrongdoing.
Contrive: To bring about by scheme, planning.

Connotation: The implied or suggested meaning of a word or phrase in addition to its explicit meaning.
Denotation: The explicit or literal meaning.

Consecutive: One following another without interruption.
Successive: One following another.

Contagious: Describes disease spread by contact.
Infectious: Describes disease spread by air or water. It may not be *contagious*.

A smile can't be *infectious* unless it's very close.

Convince: To satisfy beyond doubt by argument or evidence.
Persuade: To induce or win over by argument or entreaty.

One is convinced *of* . . . or *that* . . . , but never *to*. . . . One can be persuaded *of* . . . or *that* . . . or *to*.

Decimate: Technically, to take or destroy a tenth part of.
Destroy: To tear down, demolish, break up. Complete in itself without adding *completely*.

Malefactors with keyboards make *decimate* seem worse than it is. One alleged historian wrote that "One third of F Company was *decimated* in the action." That's about 15 soldiers. A loss, to be sure, but not crippling to the company.

Delay: Putting off in time, including a sense of hindering.
Postpone: Formally putting off, with no sense of hindering.

Discover: To find or bring forth what existed but was not known.
Invent: To create or concoct what didn't exist.

Because electrical phenomena occur in nature, nobody

could *invent* electricity. It had to be *discovered.*

Disinterested: Impartial. Not interested from selfish motive.
Uninterested: Not interested.

The *disinterested* make good judges, but not the *uninterested.*

Dispense: To give out, deal out, distribute.
Disburse: To pay out, expend.

We bend *dispense* in using the word to mean the payment of money.

Dock: An excavated basin to receive ships between voyages.
Pier: A platform built out over water from the shore.
Quay: A landing or wharf built to receive, load and unload ships.
Wharf: A platform built parallel to the shore.

The word most commonly misused here is *dock,* which clearly is a waterway rather than a construction above water.

Ecology: A study of the relationship between the environment and its organisms.
Environment: Surroundings.

Ecology, the newer word, is almost trendy in some applications and threatens to intrude into every *environment.* The latter word has become overpopular as part of catch phrases:

learning *environment*, working *environment*, etc.

Encroach: To trespass or intrude upon the rights or property of another. Used with *on* or *upon*.
Infringe: To break or violate rights, patents or sovereignty of another. Not necessary to include *on* or *upon*.

Entitled: Deserving.
Titled: Having a title. Designated by title.

Some lords and ladies, presumably, are *titled* without being *entitled*.

Envy: Discontent because of someone else's advantages.
Jealousy: Apprehension or suspicion over a rival.

Excite: To arouse the emotions.
Incite: To arouse into action.

Expect: To look for as likely to occur or appear.
Anticipate: To take action in preparation for what one *expects*.

One can *anticipate* a storm by buying a raincoat. One can *expect* a storm without spending a penny.

Faze: To disturb.
Phase: A level or stage of development.

Feasible: What can be done.
Possible: What can happen.

It is *possible* for most college freshmen to learn proper English grammar, but probably not *feasible*.

Figuratively: Metaphorically.
Literally: Virtually, actually. As is.

The scoundrel here isn't *literally*, but any writer who can't believe it means the real thing.

Finance: Verb. To support with money.
Fund: Noun. A pool or source of money.

We see *fund* as a verb everywhere, as well as *funded* for the past tense and as an adjective. Even some purists now waver on this one, but just because some words appear headed for the drain doesn't mean writers shouldn't replace the stopper.

Gender: A term in grammar to describe whether a *word* is masculine, feminine or neuter.
Sex: Used in describing whether a *person* is male or female.

Maybe *gender* strays improperly into the domain of *sex* because of writers who recoil from that simple, clear three-letter word. The phrase "to have *sex*" has come into almost general use, replacing "sexual relations."

Good: Adjective. As it should be. Better than average.
Well: Adverb. In a pleasing or desirable manner. Skillfully, expertly. Satisfactorily in regard to health.

That's all well and good, but linking verbs tangle some writers. *Good* can modify a subject after a linking verb: "She felt good." But use *well* in most references to health: "After two weeks she was reported well."

Half-mast: Reference to respectful lowering of flags to half the height of its mast on ships and at naval stations.
Half-staff: The position to which flags are lowered in respect on all other flagpoles.

Hanged: Executed by hanging.
Hung: Put up, as a picture or decoration.

Confusion erupts here because the present tense, first-person form for both verbs is *hang*. Careless writers tend to extend the past tense form *hung* (as in "put up") into the scene of the execution.

Homicide: A slaying.
Manslaughter: A homicide without planning or malice.
Murder: In most states, malicious, premeditated homicide. In some states the term includes homicide that occurs during the commission of another felony.

Use of these terms should come *after* the appropriate official charges or legal convictions. Each state's laws provide an array of variations, as in *accidental homicide* or *degrees* of *manslaughter* and *murder*.

Identified: Shown to be a certain person or thing.
Named: Given a name or title. Nominated or appointed.

We can assume that most people were named soon after birth, so we shouldn't name them again when we mean only that an identity has been clarified.

If: In the event that. Granting that. On the condition that.
Whether: If it is so that. If it happens that. In case.

If often introduces a subjunctive clause, a condition that is non-existent, hypothetical or improbable: "*If* it rains, the roads could be slippery." *Whether* usually introduces a group of possibilities: "*Whether* it rains or snows, the roads may be slippery."

Insistent: Making demands.
Persistent: Firmly continuing.

Good teachers *insist* and good students *persist*.

Instinct: The automatic response of animals.
Intuition: Knowledge gathered without the use of reason.

Lady: An old term of social distinction that has little or no use in modern writing.
Woman: Proper term for adults of female sex.
Girl: Proper term only for female child.

We should all join Kipling, who found no difference

between "The colonel's *lady* and Judy O'Grady . . . ," and refer to both as *women*. The term *girl*, when used in reference to anyone beyond childhood is degrading: "weather girl," "copy girl," "reception girl," "salesgirl." The same injunction applies to use of *boy* for anyone but a male child.

Lectern: A stand, behind which a speaker appears.
Podium or **dais**: A platform to speak from, often holding a *lectern*.

Any writer who places a speaker "behind the podium" puts that person out of reach of the microphone.

Less: A reduced *amount*, in dealing with matter that cannot be counted, as in "less grain."
Fewer: A smaller *number*, as in "fewer bushels."

Widespread use of *less* in places that call for *fewer* may arise from a sense that *fewer* seems stilted or awkward. Those writers should consider that use of *less* in such cases not only seems illiterate, it is illiterate.

Less than: A smaller number or amount.
Under: Physically below.

These can be grouped with *more than* and *over*. Because *under* has several meanings it can cause confusion.

Libel: Defamation in print, writing, record, pictures, signs or effigies.
Slander: Oral defamation.

Like: Not acceptable as a conjunction.
As or **as if**: Proper as a conjunction.

An easy rule here: *Like* takes a simple object: "It looks *like* snow." *As* and *as if* introduce a clause: "It looks *as if* it will snow," or "He took off *as* he was told."

Locate: To set or place.
Find: To uncover the place of.

Although it seems improbable, writers misuse *locate* in the sense of *find*, especially in reference to people. Also, it's redundant to use *at* with *locate* or *situate*.

Lower: In a place below another. To reduce height.
Smaller: Not as large in size.

Lower also is sometimes used improperly for *reduce*, as in price.

Majority: More than half. Refers to people or their representation by vote.
Most: The greatest amount or degree of anything.
Plurality: As in votes or voters, the largest number, even though less than half.

Most is proper most of the time, but writers seem to ignore it. Use *majority* only in counting people or their votes, not in counting rotten apples.

-mania: An abnormal enthusiasm for.
-philia: An abnormal attraction to.
-phobia: An abnormal fear of.

Military: Armed forces, not including *naval* forces.
Naval: Pertaining to the sea forces.

The error is in assuming that *military* encompasses seagoing forces. It isn't that *naval* forces aren't militant. They are, especially if lumped with *military*.

More than: A greater number or amount.
Over: Above, upon, beside, beyond, across.

Although definitions for *over* include *beyond* and *in excess,* its spatial entanglements take it out of consideration as a good synonym for *more than*. Also, it should never be used to replace *during* or *throughout*, as in, "She practiced over the weekend."

Nation: Refers to the people, not the territory.
Country: Refers to the territory.

"And crown thy good with brotherhood" refers to the *nation*. "From sea to shining sea!" refers to the *country*.

Oculist: Either an ophthalmologist or an optometrist.
Ophthalmologist: A physician who treats illnesses of the eyes.
Optician: Makes eyeglasses and may not be a physician.
Optometrist: Measures vision and prescribes eyeglasses. Need not be a physician.

These words may seem to cut super-fine distinctions laid down by specialists, but they are useful so long as clarity remains the objective.

Occur: Refers to an accidental or unscheduled event.
Take place: Refers to a planned event.

This should be a simple distinction. A plane crash *occurs*. A graduation ceremony *takes place*. A ceremony or event isn't *staged*, unless it appears on a stage or is meant only to seem real.

Opaque: Describes material that can't be seen through.
Translucent: Describes material that can't be seen through clearly.
Transparent: Describes material that can be seen through clearly.

Oral: Spoken words.
Verbal: In words, either spoken or written.

For clarity, use *oral* and *written* to make this distinction, because *verbal* can only cause confusion.

Pardon: To free one from more punishment for a crime.
Parole: To release one from prison early.
Probation: Punishment one receives other than imprisonment.

Writers probably confuse these words because they all deal with punishment in the legal system. All journalists ought to be familiar with laws in their states which might give special meaning to each word.

People: Use when referring to large groups.
Persons: Use when referring to a few or an exact number.

A *person* here and a *person* there, and before you know it, you've got a bunch of *people*.

Per: A preposition from Latin meaning *by means of, through* or *by*.
A or **an**: English prepositions or articles.

It makes little sense today to use a Latin word where good English words are clearer. Use *per* only in technical or scientific writing where it seems appropriate. Also, it sounds more natural in *per capita*, miles *per* gallon and *percent*.

Plenty: Plentiful, enough, ample.
Plethora: Too full, overabundance, excess.

Polite: Showing good manners.
Courteous: Showing kindness beyond politeness.

Politeness opens the door for a friend. *Courtesy* stands waiting in the rain with a friend for a taxi to arrive.

Presently: Soon.
Now: At this moment.

Writers tangle these in statements like this: "She is *presently* in charge of enlistments."

Prone: Face-down position.
Supine: Face-up position.

Thoughtless writers use these words to prove that they can describe the position of a body. Confused readers might wish that the writers had used *face-down* or *face-up*.

Prophesy: To foretell out of inspiration or use of the occult.
Predict: To foretell on the basis of facts.

Careless writers tend to use *prophesy* when they have no inspiration.

Ravage: To destroy or ruin.
Ravish: To rape or carry away with force.

A bad flood, then, can *ravage* a city, and a bad person can *ravish* a maiden.

Reapportion: To reform the boundaries of state legislative districts.
Redistrict: To reform the boundaries of congressional districts.

Reluctant: Not willing to act.
Reticent: Not willing to speak.

Reverend: An adjective often misused as a title for a person in a religious ministry. It is used properly to identify a minister on first reference: "The *Rev.* John Smith . . . "

Minister or **pastor**: A noun and proper title for anyone authorized to carry out the spiritual functions of a church. *Pastor, curate,* or *father* is not routinely used as an adjective with a name unless in quotations.

Round: A single shot from a weapon.
Salvo: Several shots in succession.
Volley: Several simultaneous shots.

This meaning has nothing to do with a *round* of applause, which usually comes as a *salvo*. A *round* of drinks often comes as single *shots*.

Salary: A fixed payment to a non-hourly employee.
Wages: Payment to an employee.

The world of business makes this distinction, possibly to help separate blue collars and white collars.

Subsequent: Following another, when the events are not connected.
Consequent: Following naturally, when the events are connected.

One crime can be *subsequent* to another, but punishment is normally *consequent* to the crime.

Successive: One after another.
Consecutive: Without interruption, one after another.

Surprise: To come upon unexpectedly. To take or be taken unawares.
Astonish: To fill with sudden wonder. To amaze.

Soldiers caught napping on guard duty are *surprised*. They may be *astonished* by their punishment.

Think: To form or have in the mind. To hold in one's opinion.
Believe: To take as true, real. To have trust, confidence. To hold views.
Feel: To perceive or be aware of through physical sensation.

A *belief* is more strongly held than a *thought*, so isn't precisely synonymous. One wouldn't write "I believe it will rain today." *Think* is clear, plain and simple. *Feel* should never be used in place of either *think* or *believe*, as in "He said he feels that a suit would be out of place at the picnic."

11

Sham, Scam, Puff and Fluff

There was this writer named Burke,
Who filled his stories with murk.
His editors shed tears,
And swore they lost years
In finding clear words that work.

Murk and Muddle

Murky language descends on journalists every day. Sometimes news people create foggy English themselves, and much of their information, whether from records, notes, handouts, speeches or interviews, comes to them shrouded in confusion and obscurity.

Some sources spin this cloud intentionally, but most language fog arises from failure to understand and use English well. It's every journalist's responsibility to blow away the murk and pass information along to readers with the clarity and precision the language allows.

Here we won't concern ourselves with accuracy of facts, the subject of other studies, but with common language problems that create muddled communication and with ways to purge sentences of those problems. Some faults have become so common that they threaten to force out simple and clear forms.

Many language ailments can be grouped and studied together. One doesn't resolve faults simply by giving them names, but to help understand them students of language have put tags on some elements of the muddle: *jargon, euphemism, doublespeak, gobbledegook, wordiness, cliché* and *redundancy.*

Promotional Hype and Advertising Fluff

Consider first the murk produced by design, for deception. Some may be almost innocent, relatively harmless fudgery, as in listing a janitor euphemistically as a *maintenance engineer,* calling a bus a *deluxe motorcoach* or calling a sale an *inventory reduction.* But some news sources, hoping to camouflage their poorer qualities or actions, surround them with fuzzy words, hoping the audience won't notice. They have learned that words can hide their mistakes. News people call it "blowing smoke." It becomes especially serious when the smoke blowers are public officials.

Promotional writers and editors who seek not to communicate news but to advance the best features of a product, institution, cause, or person naturally select their words for clarity and persuasion. But when inevitably they must present their clients' weak or dark sides, they select fudge words, trying to redirect or manipulate the reader's attention. Note, for example, the mumbo jumbo in presenting hair restoration as *scalp reduction,* or in insisting that used cars and other goods were *pre-owned.* Who does it help to change *solitary confinement* to *adjustment center*? Can language be too honest?

Readers should understand that these writers and editors aren't necessarily working in the readers' interests, but for clients whose objectives may not be accurate and clear communication. News people must hold out a hand to readers by translating and explaining.

Analyzing a speech written for a politician challenges the analyst and can reveal some common word manipulations. Those seeking office have swung the word *establishment* like a sword for years to wound incumbents. Nobody seems to know what the term means, although we assume it refers to "ins." Should they win, those who seek office presumably take on the same implied characteristics.

How many times have politicians used terms like *middle American, the forgotten man* and *silent majority* to try to attract voters who think their views go unnoticed? If asked, ten voters might produce ten definitions of each word, and that vagueness makes the terms attractive on the political stump. If words aren't clear, the speaker can't be pinned down or held accountable.

In politics, the challenger always proposes *real progress, to move forward, to get the economy going again, to turn this country (state or city) around, to present a new vision* (usually for the *future,* which is the best place for visions).

The speaker's opponents always *oppose new ideas and vision, obstruct those who want progress* and *represent the old and worn out.*

As with all sources, journalists should ask politicians for specific meanings.

Even the terms *public affairs* and *public relations* are euphemisms for advertising. It's natural for those who try to sell the advantages of institutions or individuals to use the techniques of those who sell products and services.

Language fog can appear on a world scale or in one's hometown. Adolph Hitler's *final solution* helped to conceal the killing of six million Jews during World War II. Americans can remember military and diplomatic leaders who called U.S. soldiers *advisers.* Soldiers killed by their own men were victims of *friendly fire.* Civilians and their property that got in the way were classified under *collateral damage.* Invasions became *incursions,* and bombings *air support.* Spying has been called *human intelligence collection.*

Back at the hometown level an airport public relations release calls a crash a *failed landing.* Department heads try to hide budgets that run into the red by calling them *shortfalls.*

Some distasteful words, like *tax increase,* turn into *revenue enhancement, investments* or *contributions.* The mayor's assistant, instead of admitting that his boss's facts were wrong, calls them *inoperative.* A downtown business calls a down payment a *capital reduction charge.*

Journalists, after years of effort, have forced funeral directors to accept the fact that people *die* and do not *pass on.* Readers still find, however, that some citizens are *laid to rest* instead of *buried.* Sexual liaisons usually hide behind the term *relationships.*

It's common to see the fudge word *terminated* instead of *fired* or *laid off,* but it can get worse. One company cut thousands of employees from its payroll and called it *involuntary force reduction.* Other firms have called it *reducing duplication* or *diminishing head count.* That presumably depersonalizes firings or elimination of jobs. On the other side of that coin, business jargon has turned job placement outside the firm into *outplacement.* Some companies who farm out production of components call it *outsourcing.*

Secret meetings of officials should be called *secret* instead of *behind closed doors.* Public officials find it easier to raise or spend public tax dollars when journalists allow them to call those dollars *funding, resources* or *appropriations.* Some officials play on the knowledge that readers might not recognize themselves if they are called *populations.*

Dazzled by handouts, journalists every day allow themselves to become *resource persons* for those who hold private or public office. Without dedicated translation by writers and editors this murk creates among readers a general feeling of deception, what has been called a "credibility gap." Unless news people clear the fog away it creates a general cynicism toward government.

Authorities Talk: Jargon of the Expert and Almost Expert

Inside Words

Journalists ought to resist the real or devised words specialists use to communicate among themselves. News people, not usually schooled in law, medicine, education, the natural or social sciences, encounter jargon because they often depend on specialists to provide facts and background explanation for events. News people must interview many others who aren't professionals: policemen, public officials, computer programmers, even plumbers.

It's one thing to interview a specialist. It's another matter, however, to pass along to readers information that still drips with the specialist's jargon. Reporters, left in specialized beats too long, have been known to adopt the language of their sources. It's any reporter's or editor's duty to identify and translate words which may mean something to the source but little to readers.

Some specialists, though usually not pompous, are proud of their "inside" words and have resisted attempts to translate them. In such cases it's best to make these sources into allies, enlisting them in the cause of clarity. If that fails, reporters must advise their sources that their information won't see print unless they clarify terms in question.

Some language fluff comes to reporters from those who have become addicted to adding the suffix *-wise* to nouns. They produce a language swagger that strangles meaning, as in *budget-wise* or *tax-wise*. Those efforts fail, *information-wise.*

Murky Medics

One wouldn't expect a journalist to repeat a medical doctor's use of *myocardial infarction* without translating it as *heart attack*. But that technical term has appeared undecoded in many newspapers, along with hundreds of other expressions equally murky to newspaper readers. For example, a doctor may call anything from a seizure to a fainting spell an *episode*. The term *procedure* blankets every operation from brain surgery to stitching a cut finger. Doctors call medical treatment a *protocol*. When medical people become specific they often speak or write in terms of *syndromes* and *disorders,* as in *attention-deficit disorder* or *post-traumatic stress disorder*. Writers, and ultimately editors, must get answers to their questions in order to translate and present precise information clearly.

Academic Psychobabble

Modern academic jargon, often called academese and psychobabble, has invaded nearly every classroom from kindergarten through the university. Much of this compulsion to use smoke and mirrors can be laid to enthusiasm that has evaded the discipline of language.

Some observers of this phenomenon, often students of academicians who use the words, suspect that they simply cover old ideas in new paint. Whole sentences often defy comprehension. Interviewing in some halls of academia a reporter enters a minefield of murk, popularly called "buzzwords" by those who haven't fallen victim. Here is a sentence to tangle the most literate reader.

> One conceptualization integrates a systematized incremental programming.

Unchecked by logic and language sense, those who spin such webs of fog have tried to replace good words with strange creations. Computer systems may swallow such doublespeak without ill effect, but not people. Some of these creations undoubtedly result from a misguided groping for elegance. One college street demonstrator said in an impromptu interview.

> "Everybody was motivated to make a positive impact."

Outwardly unchanged, classrooms have become *learning space,* perhaps to convince taxpayers of their efficiency. Good teachers are often caught *reinforcing positive behavior.* Libraries have become *media resource centers. Interaction* has taken over from meeting and talking. Personnel offices have turned into *human resource centers.*

Anyone who helps has become a *facilitator.* Everything seems to start at *square one.* Anything positive has turned into *proactive.* Activities now must be *initiatives.* Expensive consumer goods are *high end.* New ideas are on the *cutting edge.* Anything more complicated than a light bulb is *high tech.* All new machines are *state-of-the-art.* Anything not visible is *in-depth.* Anything ranging from alive to acceptable is now *viable.* Health has become *wellness,* raising children has become *parenting* and family life has turned into *familyness.* Anything that fails, from family to institution, has become *dysfunctional.* It isn't enough for prices or problems to rise. They must *escalate.*

Mechanics have become *service technicians.* Any chance is a *window of opportunity.* When we study anything today we *get a read* on it, *monitor* it or *factor it in.* If we understand, or find a solution, we *get a handle* on it. When we reject an idea *we don't buy it.* If we prepare to take action we *go with it,* then we *get up to speed* so we can *hit the ground running.*

One doesn't listen to or watch a performance. One *experiences* it. We no longer absorb information. We *internalize* it. We don't get out. We *egress.* We no longer eat, drink or inhale. We *ingest.*

Vogue Words

Much of what fills the world's memo pads is trendiness instead of jargon. These vogue words and phrases may hang around a while, pass through the cliché stage and then leave as quickly as they appeared. Here is a small collection.

Business people who are *heavy hitters* and do things *big*

time, are *players* and *into* fad words. They seek the *bottom line* for the *near term* or until they see *how it will play out* and can *cut a deal.* They ask their accountants to *interface* with inventory and *cost it out* in order to *optimize the cash flow. Up-front* teachers ask their *cool* or *uncool* students to *listen up* to *gut-level feedback* if they don't want to be *out of it.* If they decide not to *split,* and if they *target* an *upscale lifestyle,* those students will *go with the flow* and learn *where they're coming from. Disincentives,* although real *bummers,* keep *task forces on target* toward *commonalities.* The *high profile* leader is *up-tight,* and even *hung up,* but his *charisma triggers* an *on-going input* for a *positive impact,* which leads to more *Mickey Mouse.* Everybody seems to be *chilled out* and *gearing up* to *hammer out* a new *scenario* before it's *history.*

Little wonder that readers *max out* or *freak out.* They may feel *ripped off* and *stressed out.* It's time for a *reality check.*

Reporters and editors can't help but suspect that administrators who refer to *interpersonal dialogue* probably can't think or speak clearly themselves. Similarly, those who say they *prioritize* their work may not accomplish much.

It may sound fresher or kinder to an educator to call it *mainstreaming* when referring to placement of a physically or mentally handicapped student in a class of students without handicap. The term dumps confusion on readers instead of freshness unless the news writer explains it.

Police Blotter Fog

Police jargon, usually a mix of legal terminology, police blotter fog and the tired words of social workers and insurance writers, is enough to make the angels weep. A misdirected concern by some police officers for rights of the accused can create a deadly effect on readers. A reporter who talks to an officer at the scene may get a statement like this.

> "The intoxicated subject was apprehended on the premises when he exited the vehicle."

In describing what an unidentified wrongdoer did at a crime scene, police often use the foggy catch-alls *perpetrator* and *party* or, even worse, *suspect.* Writers should know that an unidentified person cannot logically be a *suspect,* and use of the word after identification invites a libel suit if the person hasn't been charged. Both police and police reporters lean precariously on the word *allegedly* in the hope that it will protect them legally if they are sued. It won't.

Twisting Nouns Into Verbs

Trace a share of language abuse to attempts to make nouns into verbs. Some of these verbal transformations come with no change in spelling.

To access. *Gain access, enter* or *use* provide precise meaning.

To advantage. Better to *provide an advantage.*

To author. *Write* is better.

To bus. Why not *send by bus*?

To chair. *Lead* or *direct* are better and avoid the problem sexist word *chairman.* Almost any form is better than *to head up.*

To contact. Use *call, write* or *visit.*

To craft. Why not *make*?

To critique. The verb is *criticize.*

To dialogue. Make it *talk* or *discuss.*

To fault. Better to use *criticize* or *find fault.*

To gift. Make it *give.*

To headquarter. *Has headquarters in* is clearer.

To host. *Have* or *hold* are better.

To impact. *Affect* is better.

To interface. *Meet, talk, gather, connect,* etc., are more precise.

To jet. *Fly* does it all.

To leverage. *To take (or use) advantage* is better.

To liaise. Why not *communicate?*

To market. Better to use *advertise* or *sell,* as appropriate.

To network. *Organize, cooperate* or *circulate* are better, as appropriate.

To package. *Put together* or *prepare* are clearer.

To parent. *Raise* is better.

To premiere. *To hold a premiere* is clearer.

To service. *To assist, repair* or *fulfill* are good.

To target. *Aim at* is better.

To task. Better to write *assign* or *require.*

To trash. *Criticize, ruin* or *destroy,* where appropriate, are more precise.

Changing Words to Make Verbs

One trendy tack has added *-ize* to words, thus "verbizing" them. The pretentious practice gets out of hand and produces bureaucratic barbarisms.

> He was asked to *finalize* his plans.

> The general *prioritized* his schedule.

> The doctor *institutionalized* her patient.

> The class *optimized* its grades.

> The attack plan *maximized* its chances for success.

> He agreed to *utilize* his gardening skills.

> She wanted to *accessorize* her new outfit.

It's popular, but improper, to add the prefix *re-* to words like *affirmed, doubled, shuffled* and *stated* without first making certain that the affirming, doubling, shuffling and stating already has occurred once.

12

Signs of Wear

There was a writer named Cutter,
Who caused his teacher to mutter:
"I've read this, all right,
But the effect is much like
Wading in peanut butter."

Tired Words in Sports

Sports, both those involving popular participation and varieties performed before audiences, have produced a rich language that struggles every day to free itself from a bog of cliché and jargon. Unfortunately, sports writers often inflict the lingo of coaches and players on readers who would appreciate a helping hand. Both writers and editors who handle sports copy ought to try to broaden understanding of the games, and thus readership, by explaining the terms. Too often they appear to discourage entrance of the uninitiated into ranks of the aficionados.

Stories about basketball might well carry the notice to readers: "If you don't understand what *setting a pick* means, or *charging the lane*, leave us and turn to the comics page." Players are too often *hacked in the act* when they are *in the paint*.

The following bits of jargon have become clichés and can be found in nearly every sports section, every football season.

Worthwhile teams nearly always engage in *one game at a*

time. They all *come to play.*

Passing quarterbacks either *drop back in the pocket* or *scramble.* If they are worth their salt they have *good speed, good hands* and *quick feet.* When these folks *air it out* they create *bullets* or *frozen ropes.* They might even *unload a bomb.*

A good ball carrier must *read his keys* and may *charge the line* or *run wide* and try to *turn the corner.*

A good pass receiver is a *deep threat* and *glue-fingered,* and can *burn* the cornerback. He *finds the crease,* runs a *buttonhook,* a *comeback,* a *corner, post, Z-streak* or a *fly pattern.* He might encounter a *dime back.*

Opponents may look tough, but usually get into their pants *one leg at a time.*

All coaches come prepared with *game plans* and try to get their teams *up for the contest.* Each coach tries to present a *new look* for the opposition.

Audiences, always "fans," affect the outcome by getting *into* the game (or not).

If a team hasn't *coughed the ball up* it might add to its *W* stats. Zero is *zip* and a tie is *a wash.*

Losers are always *class guys* but, you see, didn't *execute* well enough, *establish the running game* or *follow the game plan.*

It's time for sports writers and editors to examine every word for signs of wear. Fresh terminology can be like oxygen to readers. If writers and editors think their hard-core followers would object to fresher terms or explanations of terms in stories, they might consider periodically offering soft-core or potential readers a separate collection of terms and definitions. They could surprise themselves by uncovering a wider audience.

Legal Obfuscation

Legal terminology, presumably of value in legislation, court records and communication among attorneys, has no place in a news story without translation. Latin words form much of the spine on which the profession hangs new bones every day. Also, the legal meaning of some English words differs from their normal meaning. Reporters and editors should never stray far from a law dictionary or fail to ask an attorney to define the legalese.

Military and Naval Doubletalk

Some who write armed services news releases have carried doubletalk to absurd lengths. Although these faults aren't limited to them they commonly join their words, making prepositions the prefixes to verbs, as in *ongoing*, *downsize*, *offload* and *overfly*. The catch-all terms *ordnance* and *resources* too often blanket more specific terms like bombs, rockets, shells and bullets. Nothing in the armed services seems to be sent or distributed. It's all *deployed*. Even yes and no become *affirmative* and *negative*.

Another favorite of service news conferences often finds its way into published news stories. It's the technique of making a key noun an adjective to modify another adjective, thus omitting an entire phrase.

> The airfield was described as *C-5 capable*.

> Uniforms couldn't be *gas-prepared* in the time available.

> New pay policies became *personnel-effective* within two months.

Some verb constructions in the services go beyond the ridiculous. The following may stand the momentary test of convenience, but not that of toleration.

To attrit. Used instead of *to reduce*.
To configure. Used for *to arrange*, as in parts or outline.

To credential. Used for *to identify*.
To degrade. Used for *to damage*.
To incent. Used for *to encourage*.
To surveille. Used for *to watch*.

Clichés

Some expressions we see every day started their careers as bright writing. That's why they caught on, became popular and ultimately wore out. Writers who don't read as much as they should will fail to recognize and discard them. Continued use of these tired words tends to make whole stories and the information in them seem old. They number in the thousands, but here are a few of the tiredest.

shots rang out	coveted trophy
pulled out all the stops	given a green light
behind closed doors	fell on deaf ears
followed in the wake of	got into full swing
blanket of snow	few and far between
dig in their heels	down to earth
bone of contention	cold as ice
by leaps and bounds	crack of dawn
basked in glory	bite the bullet
come under fire	

Why should

awakenings	always be	rude
votes		crucial or mustered
silences		deafening
inquiries		far-reaching
gains		sweeping
tides		rising
desires		burning
situations		assessed

sagas	gripping
halts	grinding
ranks	closing
positions	firm
steps	preliminary
criticisms	harping
actions	triggered
problems	in hosts
convictions	spelled out
gatherings	top-level
rumors	branded as false
secrecy	official
rescues	daring
reports	fragmentary
truces	uneasy
observers	seasoned
galls	unmitigated
spleens	vented
liars	pathological
rain or snow	on tap
colors	flying
estimates	in ballparks
victories	garnered
infernos	raging
welcomes	with open arms
dialogues	meaningful
retreats	beaten and hasty
exchanges	heated
memories	fond
growths	by leaps and bounds
conditions	marginal
duos	dynamic
ovations	rousing
laurels	rested upon
parents	proud

Those who train themselves to recognize such exhausted words and phrases should be sharp enough to produce their own bright expressions, which lazy writers can then pounce upon and wear out.

Overstatement (Too Much Flash)

Writers too often try to add life to their sentences by throwing in words they think are exciting. In doing so they may only overstate the case. *Dreadful* appears where there's no *dread*. *Frightful* shows up where there's no *fright*.

Words that describe and modify, whether adjectives, adverbs or verbs, ought to go no further than accuracy allows.

Here is a short list of overwrought flash words that can create more heat than light.

angry	grim
assail	hammered
awesome	holocaust
blast	massive
bloody	rampage
breakthrough	reveal
brutal	rip
charge	scurry
confront	shatter
crisis	slam
devastate	stalk
dump	sweep
explosive	terror
flare	

Stunting With Words

A few writers in every newsroom habitually dredge up a pompous word when readers need one that's real, clear and simple. Here's a short list of words that shouldn't appear in news copy, followed by words to use instead.

advent—arrival
aforementioned—that, those
albeit—but
ascertain—find out
coequal—equal
consummate—finish
contusion—bruise
copious—plentiful
corpulent—fat
edifice—building
effectuate—cause
enhance—improve
expedite—speed
imbibe—drink
incarcerate—jail
interrogate—question
in lieu of—instead of

initial—first
laceration—cut
lucid—clear
mendacious—lying
modicum—some
necessitates—requires
peruse—read, examine
plethora—overabundance
ponder—consider
purloin—steal
putative—supposed
reside—live
submit—send
subsequent—later
substantial—big
ultimate—final
veracity—truth

Weasel Words

Some words have no specific meaning or have lost meanings they may have had. Incredibly, the word *meaningful* is one. Writers usually can remove vague words without changing the sense of a statement. Even so, readers see such terms everywhere, which means that writers and editors haven't become sensitive to them.

The word *facility*, for example, has the vague definition of "a convenience." *Area, complex, unit* and *center* are nearly as bad, and *infrastructure* threatens to become the supreme titleholder. These words don't add meaning even when writers throw in other nouns to try to modify them.

A *highway facility* could mean almost anything. The writer should look for the right term: bridge, culvert, interchange, and so forth. A *hospital facility* could be anything from an operating room to a bedpan. A *learning facility* could be anything from a library to a pad of paper.

Some writers have developed a habit of adding the word *situation* as a vague noun, modified by a more precise noun which should stand alone.

> **Wrong:** The game is in an overtime *situation*.
> **Right:** The game is in overtime.

> **Wrong:** Police report a hostage *situation*.
> **Right:** Police report a hostage has been taken.

Popular but imprecise modifiers like *very, quite, really, actually, definitely, basically, seriously, totally, kind of* and *sort of* also should alert journalists. They must recognize fog, if not evasiveness, in these words and challenge sources who use them.

The words *very* and *quite*, of course, are redundant if used with words absolute in themselves: *very* unique, *quite* final.

The *Work With* Habit

Few weasel words have created the mischief of *work with*. It has spread from conversational English to popular and academic writing. Both writers and readers appear to slide over it, not recognizing the lack of substance. Here are some examples.

> Her duty was to *work with* second graders. (Readers might ask, "What does she *do* with second graders?")

> The mayor and her aides *worked with* developers to plan adequate park space. (That's redundant. Why not write, "The mayor, her aides and developers planned for adequate park space.")

Contradicting and Nonsense Terms

We burden our language unnecessarily by using terms that cancel themselves out through contradiction. Here are some examples.

calm winds   a swift end
centered around   a definite possibility
a new tradition   turned up missing.
a near miss

Other terms make no sense as used. Sports writers have made a cliché of *untracked* to mean out of a rut and back on the scoring path. Sports writers also habitually use the word *recruited* to mean a player was pursued for membership on a team whether signed or not. Armed services recruiters would like permission to count their recruits that way.

Many nonsense phrases have become a part of idiomatic English and will be with us as long as we can use them, though they express impossible or awkward conditions.

put one's *best* foot forward
turned a deaf ear
to the ends of the earth
the player lucked out
watch your head
head over heels in love
speaking tongue in cheek

Idioms Off the Track

Though many idioms have been with us for a century or more they can add to language fog when writers cripple their construction.

The wrong preposition can stretch an idiom out of shape.

Experienced writers develop an ear for the right one. Here are examples of idioms bent or broken by their prepositions.

He *died from* cholera in 1913. (Make it *died of.*)

Her hair was *different than* Mary's. (*Different from* is better.)

His ball was *identical to* Jim's. (*Identical with* is better.)

She was *persuaded that* . . . (Make it *persuaded to.*)

She was *pleased with* the letter. (*Pleased by* is better.)

He became concerned when a man leaned *out* the passenger window. (Should be *from.*)

The I-back gained 788 yards *on* the season. (Should be *during.*)

He decided to speak *to* his nephew. (Make it speak *with.*)

Her office was independent *from* the university. (Make it independent *of.*)

The lieutenant ordered an investigation *into* the shooting. (Make it investigation *of.*)

13

Tightening the Writing

There was a writer named Bryce
Who had to say everything twice.
He knew 'twas redundant,
But his words were abundant.
Now he is trying for thrice.

Too Many Words

Modern newspaper readers must select from thousands of messages that fly at them every day. It makes sense that in preparing those messages writers and editors delete words and phrases that don't add to information or understanding. Newspapers sell space, so this paring, in addition to saving the reader's time, saves money for the newspaper publisher, who sells space. It's an old newsroom expectation for good writers or editors to save space that would sell for dollars equal to their own salaries. Tight writing and editing takes time. It's harder. It's also crucial if journalists are to help readers.

Redundancy

Some writers accept the notion that if one word works, two work better. Although repetition may succeed as a teaching technique it only steals space from a journalist. If writers shouldn't repeat words they also shouldn't use words together that even imply the same meaning. As Yogi Berra is reported to have said, "It's déjà vu all over again." It's a kind of fat writing, and it signals the writer's ineptness.

Most writers and editors can recognize the more obvious kinds of redundancies. They appear in print every day.

free gifts	true facts
past history	old adages
future plans	may possibly
completely destroyed	advance warning
added bonus	quoted as saying
priceless treasures	twirled around
dived down	ascended up
referred back	wavered back and forth
typical example	unverified rumor
first started	retreated back
new record	trained expert
pedestrian walkway	well-known celebrity
to share together	new innovation
reflect back	this type (anything)
each and every	rules and regulations
fight against	to both agree
cease and desist	end result
continue on	reduce down

It requires some thought to recognize these pairs. They not only eat space, but continued use threatens the meaning of the base word. *Gifts,* standing alone, are *free,* but readers who constantly see the two words together may conclude that *gifts,* indeed, are not free unless accompanied by that extra word. That erodes meaning from *gifts.* Some redundancies are less obvious and must be dug out of more complex sentence forms (unneeded words in italics).

learn to walk *all over* again.
an autopsy *to determine cause of death*
no protection *at all*
where we are *at*
that's *the reason* why
three *different* views turned up
the plane plummeted *to the ground below*
partners in a business *together*
debating one *possible* proposal
Speaking to the gathered governors on Monday he said . . .
they learned to coexist *with each other*
no reports *whatsoever*
mothers *pre*planned their activities
some began to *un*loosen their ties

Here's an example of super-redundancy.

They started to plan *ahead for the future*.

Wordiness in Phrases

Tightening one's own writing or the writing of others includes looking for simple, single words that can replace entire phrases without subtracting meaning.

in the not too distant future—soon
as a consequence of—because
at the conclusion of—after
at this point in time—now
despite the fact that—although
take a look at—examine
in the event that—if
take into consideration—consider
give emphasis to—emphasize
prepare a list of—list
take a hammer and hit—hammer
make a decision—decide

come up with—produce
take a leadership role—lead
were in attendance—attended
in its entirety—all
put an end to—stop
on the rise—rising
one on one—personal
on an interim basis—temporarily

General Modifiers

General modifiers add so little meaning writers can delete them or replace them with more specific terms. Descriptions of size or measure, especially, depend so much on comparison or relationship that they must be replaced by the precise. Instead of writing about a *gigantic* stadium, for example, a reporter might tell readers how many spectators it seats. News people should throw out vague adjectives like *big, huge, massive, diminutive, unprecedented* and *vast*. Instead, they should try offering readers a comparison, try describing what their subject is like.

Length and Pretense

Sometimes the length and pretense of words can produce their own deadly effect on writing. Journalists, after all, should write to express, not to impress. On occasion a long word brings a specific meaning no other provides and should hold its ground. But writers usually can find a shorter, simpler word that's exactly right. Most big words are not as familiar to readers, who may pause or even stop reading entirely when they encounter the unfamiliar.

Choosing the simple and clear often means selecting the shorter word. Simply counting words and syllables in sentences can't make one a good writer, but it can help. Readability formulas and indexes usually start with numbers of syllables. When news sources use long, complicated words, reporters and editors have a responsibility to translate them, jargon or not. Writers who want to be clear use

buy	rather than	purchase
use		utilize
end		finalize
yes		affirmative
get		acquire
try		attempt
aid		assist
job		employment
cut		lacerate
do		implement
pay		remunerate
make		fabricate
no		negative

14

Bias in Words

There was a writer named Knight,
Who had no ambition to fight.
He tried to be fair,
But lacking much care,
His words all leaned to the right.

Cultural and Social Change

Words, like people, come loaded with all kinds of baggage. We know that words can carry more than one meaning according to how and where we use them, but awkward as that can be, it's the easy part. Those immersed in English discover every day that while the language always changes it hasn't always shifted fast enough to stay abreast of other cultural and social changes. We also learn that many individuals haven't changed their attitudes to keep up with such changes.

Few journalists try to make their word choices offensive or demeaning to anybody. Most are proud of their efforts to keep up with developments and attitudes of the day, making certain, especially, that their words are fair in all respects to women, the elderly, the handicapped and members of all races as well as to individuals and their groups.

But here's where centuries of culturally biased laws and education combine with centuries of culturally biased language to thwart our best intentions. Our laws treated whole races as potential slaves, women as adjuncts to men. Our education, especially deficient for centuries in information about women and all minorities, still places a subtle twist on what we write. Our language has been enriched, yes, but is still burdened by having grown out of tongues that reflected older cultural influences. This has created further hazards. Fair and fresh reporting of a world slowly becoming enlightened demands that all journalists understand biases imprinted on our words and on us as individuals.

The grand cultural transformation of the Twentieth Century slowly changed laws, practices and attitudes that grew from old presumptions. If journalists are to be an effective part or leaders of that change, they must study their language and help change it where it has failed to be real, let alone fair.

Sexism

Journalists ought to be aware of how the careless use of language in newswriting can continue to spread subtle presumptions they may not know they have regarding women. Here are ways to avoid making a news story sexist.

1. Don't identify a person as a woman in a story unless you would identify a person in a similar position as a man. The key is to ask what makes a person's sex newsworthy.

> Police reported answering a call from a man who complained that a woman neighbor had thrown garbage over his fence into his garden. (Why aren't they just *residents* and *neighbors?*)

2. Women have their own identities. Don't identify a woman through her relationship to a man unless that relationship itself is news.

A fund drive leader said John Q. Jones, a Midtown dentist, contributed $1,500 over the weekend, and the dentist's wife contributed an equal amount.

3. A woman's dress or appearance should not be newsworthy unless the story is about clothing styles or makeup, or the story includes information about the dress or appearance of men.

Diane Olson, a stunning blond and the third witness for the defense, appeared in a tight, short satin dress.

4. It encourages stereotyping to consider a woman's achievements in the professions or in business more unusual than those of men, or more newsworthy than achievements as a mother and homemaker.

The candidates met in the afternoon with career women at the Mission Art Gallery and later met at the homes of several housewives and mothers.

5. A woman's marital status rarely carries real news value, so don't give it any precedence.

Of the six persons testifying at the flood-control hearing, two were women and both said they were married.

6. Don't use *he, him, his* as generics when referring to an antecedent noun of unknown gender.

The newspaper editor usually could provide a good background on his town.

Using *him or her,* or *his or hers,* etc., grows tiresome and awkward, however, so it helps to use plural pronouns (*they, their,* etc.) and plural antecedents. The sentence cited as sexist above, for example, could have been written like this:

Newspaper *editors* usually could provide a good background on *their* towns.

The search for a singular personal pronoun without gender almost certainly will produce a new pronoun. Please note that the word *gender* applies only to *words*, and *sex* refers to *people*, *animals* and *plants*.

7. Don't use demeaning terms to describe women.

Gals	sexpots
girls	damsels in distress
broads	helpless females
blondes	sweethearts
honeys	dolls
the little woman	babes
first lady	chicks
little lady	

8. Don't use courtesy titles for women (*Miss, Mrs., Ms.*) but not for men. Instances in which titles are necessary would seem to require a return to titles in every reference.

9. Be consistent and equal in referring to men and women.

Instead of	do this
Sam Olson and Miss Means	Sam Olson and Mary Means
Mary and Olson	Mary and Sam
Mr. Olson and Mary	Olson and Means
man and wife	husband and wife

Sexist Words

Some words come loaded with stereotypical and sexist connotation. It's best to find words free of gender even if it means using longer terms or reconstructing sentences.

Most obvious sexist words are those mentioned above or those built around the word *man*, as in *ad man*, *craftsman*, or *fathers*, as in *forefathers*. These don't include even half the population. An acceptable universal term usually can be substituted for most *man* terminology when describing people of both sexes.

When referring to a woman, the word *woman* (*chairwoman*, etc.) makes a good substitute. The word *person* has had its innings but lacks acceptability because it is simply unwieldy: *foreperson*, *henchperson*, *countryperson*, etc. Another failure has been the use of *chair* to replace *chairman*. It seems absurd to call a person of either sex a *chair* in the interest of fairness.

In justice to both sexes it would be best for all journalists to remove the "gender letters" imposed on some words through their foreign origins.

aviatrix
blonde
brunette
coed
divorcee
executrix

fiancee
heroine
poetess
sculptress
waitress

Racism and Other -isms

Few journalists today, whatever their origin or background, would contend that their own ethnic stock is superior to others or admit that they discriminate against other ethnic or racial groups. Blatant racial and ethnic slurs are hard to find in most newspapers. Still, stereotypical words and subtle racial slights appear in news stories regularly. Much of this can be explained by the general lack of awareness of our own racial and cultural biases.

These biases toward minority ethnic and racial groups and the perceptions that cause them build easily in any society through generations of neglect. No personal, let alone cultural, sensitivity regarding a minority has a chance to build when the minority remains invisible, when it is regarded as inferior or of no consequence. The social sciences finally are giving diverse racial and cultural groups their due recognition.

Several decades of political reform in much of what has been called the "free world" has brought recognition of minority rights in line with the promises found in national constitutions. The struggle to change personal and social perceptions likely will continue for further decades. Education, both formal and personal, drives much of this change, and journalists must be in front of it with encouragement and example.

Some Words Need Testing

Ability and achievement by any minority person or group, for example, should never be treated in a news story in a way that gives even the slightest impression that such ability is unusual. Many newspaper editors have trapped themselves into patronizing a minority group by "doing these folks a favor." The test of news value in *any* story involving minorities should be, Would we cover this event and use a story if the person or persons were *white males*?

This test should go beyond the choice of story to the choice of words. Referring to a person as "an *eminent* black judge" makes no sense unless it would be used in reference to a white judge with a similar record.

Some words carry with them a load of bias that is unacceptable to sensitive readers. *Minority* in itself doesn't say much. The *minority* in one country or one town may be a majority in another country or town. For example, elderly people are lumped with minorities for many considerations, but constitute a majority in many communities and may become a majority of the nation. As it is often used, the word can imply that the person or group is substandard.

Culturally deprived and *disadvantaged* are also judgmental because they imply that a standard of acceptability has been set, and this person or group doesn't measure up.

Nonwhite implies that someone has made white the standard.

MONOLITHIC NONSENSE

A common cause of unfair treatment of *any* minority group has been a tendency of writers to consider their groupings monolithic. One's sex, race, national origin, age or physical disabilities shouldn't place one automatically and forever in a mold with everyone else fitting those descriptions.

It makes little sense, for example, to assume that all blacks are poor and live in a poor area of the city. Not all women are homemakers. Not all Native Americans are from the same tribe and follow the same cultural practices. Not all people over 65 years old sit on their porches and rock. Not all disabled people are outside the thinking, working world. Each person has an identity and abilities apart from the rest.

Most journalists with any experience are aware of terminology unacceptable to women, the aged and racial, ethnic and religious minorities. They don't use those words when they have other choices. Equally important, they don't allow speakers or other newsmakers to use those words *unless the words themselves constitute the news.* In most cases unacceptable terms can be removed and the entire statement paraphrased.

It's important that in rewriting and updating their stylebooks for fairness and reality journalists maintain practical control over words. Every group with a cause seems to want to rewrite the English language, but not all causes and demands are reasonable. Without question, some proposals would replace clear, forceful terms with others more dedicated to the particular cause than to communication.

For example, journalists should use with care the words *handicapped* and *disabled,* but some groups would remove them from news pages. Anyone who reads the federal Americans With Disabilities Act can imagine the restriction such removal would place on writing.

OTHER CONNOTATIONS

Many words used by news sources and even journalists wear masks. They come with deeply hidden implications and are editorial at best. All writers and editors ought to watch for them.

Admit carries connotations of giving in reluctantly to pressure and shouldn't appear in stories where pressure doesn't exist.

> The mayor *admitted* that the city's sewer system is 90 years old and will need much repair.

Never use *bureaucrat* as a synonym for civil servants, officials or state employees.

Claim implies doubt and shouldn't appear in place of *say* or *assert.* Use *claim* properly in a legal sense when a person requests a disputed right.

> His attorney *claimed* that the easement gave him a right to use the entrance.

Innovative is both a fad word and one that implies desired change. Many proposed changes are questionable and can be challenged. Stay with *change, new methods,* etc.

Loophole comes larded with deviousness. Don't use the word when referring to people who follow standard legal steps.

Pointed out and *emphasized* as verbs of attribution leave the impression that the writer (hence the newspaper) agrees with the statement. In the interest of neutrality, use *said.*

Reform reeks with editorial implications of improvement. Politicians, especially, like the word, but reporters have no idea whether proposals wrapped in that word are any good. One person's *reform* can ruin others. Use *change* or *revision* instead.

Refute isn't synonymous with *rebut, argue, counter* or *respond to*. It means to *disprove* an argument. It's unfair and editorial to use it improperly.

Straightforward, or any other adjective that takes sides, should never describe a position, speech or action that can be questioned.

Only and *still* can put a judgmental spin on words they modify, making it appear that the reporter has taken sides.

Other words carry connotations writers may not want in their stories. One word, like *activist,* may carry the message, even the pride, of a participant. An opposition group may use another word, *militant,* which carries a pejorative connotation to describe the same person.

4

The News Story

15

Lead and Transition Faults

There was a writer named Fred,
Whose leads were invariably dead.
His words failed to show
What folks need to know
In earning their daily bread.

Lead Faults

Answering Questions

Good newswriting is hard work. It involves searching not only into the story subject but into the right way to present the news with clarity and energy. Those who have written and edited news stories for decades usually have determined that the best stories are simple tales told simply. But achieving both simplicity and readability proves more difficult than it might seem. Just as movie-goers shouldn't be aware of background music and camera techniques, readers shouldn't be distracted by the writing.

Good writers worry about readers while working on a story and try to put themselves in their shoes. They *understand* their stories. They have kept abreast of what has been published on a subject and ask if the reader would want to know about this development or be interested in that one. They ask themselves constantly if facts are relevant and necessary, if sentences are clear, if information is organized, if it holds together and makes sense without further explanation. Finally, after getting a story on paper, a good writer checks the story to see if all the reader's questions have been answered.

Leads That Don't Lead

Deadlines press against reporters as they search for that vivid collection of words to introduce a story. A good lead is one that *works*, and while it can be of any practical length, the first sentence is the most important. One either informs or interests readers right away or not at all. In writing it the author keeps two words uppermost: *Who cares?*

For that first sentence the writer needs words of mirror clarity that will share something of value without introducing muddle. First words must be strong and compelling lest the reader turn the page. Finally, those words must accurately portray the people, ideas and actions being covered.

That responsibility shouldn't overwhelm anyone committed to newswriting. All journalists should know that a dedication to news carries with it a devotion to accuracy, clarity and completeness.

They should. Often it appears that they don't. It's as important to express ideas as to produce them, but while glorifying the idea maker our society hasn't always rewarded clear expression. Sometimes it appears that nobody can produce even an understandable set of instructions for a new product.

That may explain why dull and ambiguous words fill so many news stories. Reporters who aren't encouraged to write forcefully and clearly will continue to turn off readers. News and copy editors who don't identify writing problems and send stories back to reporters have forgotten their responsibilities to those readers.

VACANT LEADS

The worst leads fail either to inform or to excite. Sometimes they tell readers what doesn't interest them.

> Mayor Arlen Jones spoke to a gathering of young civics students Tuesday night.

Hard to find a pulse there. Who cares? The mayor spoke, but *what did he say?* The lead would have caught the attention of an audience and supplied information if the writer had written it this way.

> High school students should jump into politics early by helping candidates in their campaigns, Mayor Arlen Jones told a civics class Tuesday night.

FAULTY PRIORITY

Reporters usually have collected a pile of information in their notes for a story. Searching those notes for the very best beginning sentence challenges both news sense and language skill. Some newspaper leads fail because their writers couldn't distill the best words for that first sentence. Maybe the reporter led with the *actor* when the *action* clearly had priority.

> Gov. John Milburn on Tuesday gave the legislature his five-point proposal to revise the state income tax code, shifting 20 percent of the middle-income load to those making more than $80,000 a year.

Off the mark? Sure, but that lead or its twin disgraces reporters and newspapers every day. Worse, leads like that cause readers to turn the page. The first 19 words mean nothing to those who want to know how the governor's plan affects them. This lead tells them directly and concisely.

> Middle-income taxpayers would get a 20 percent break under a proposal Gov. John Milburn gave the legislature Tuesday.

WE'VE GOT NEWS, BUT . . .

Far too many stories may as well announce in their leads that, "We've got news for you on this subject, but you'll have to read a while to get it." Here's an example.

> Rep. Jim Burbach broke his long silence Thursday on the subject of a constitutional amendment changing the way the state supplies health care for the indigent.

The summary bug has fatally bitten any reporter who turns out such nonsense. Victimized readers usually must wrestle through two or three paragraphs to learn what the news source *said* or *did*. It would be better to find a solid *theme* and get that news in the lead.

> A constitutional amendment to guarantee health care for the indigent will appear on the November ballot, Rep. Jim Burbach announced Thursday.

TOO FULLY PACKED

Other leads shoehorn far too much information into the lead sentence. Too many actors, ideas and actions overwork a reader. Instead of one clean shot of information the audience gets a double-barreled scattergun blast.

> WASHINGTON—The Department of Justice's internal watchdog unit has begun an intensive review of allegations that evidence was withheld or mishandled by department investigators who conducted separate high-profile investigations of a suspected Nazi concentration camp guard and of a collaborator, the Hastings Clarion has learned.

The writer should have tried to synthesize the story in a brief first paragraph and then filled in with further information in the next paragraph.

The Department of Justice is investigating its own investigators in the case of suspected Nazi collaborator Ivan Demjanjuk, the Hastings Clarion has learned.

The department is reviewing allegations that evidence was withheld or mishandled by those who investigated the former U.S. citizen who is appealing his war crimes conviction.

LEADS THAT ENTICE

Such leads that paint the action, however, while often effective, provide only one gateway to a story. Some leads hit readers in the eye. Others wink and jab them in the ribs. Some stories, including features, have no strong news "peg" to attract readers, but effective writers know they can grab the reader's attention anyway. Words that entice and excite, if used legitimately and accurately, get readers into stories before they know it. Such leads come from reporters who read constantly and know what words can do. Here are a few examples.

Firefighter Jim Hogan went to the right address, wrong fire.

It was the winter of Mayor Hansen's discontent.

This little boy wasn't blue but he blew his horn—until help came.

"Give me an audience and five minutes. I'll raise all the support you need," says Bill Whitley.

Leads like those should never sacrifice clarity on the altar of cuteness. They can grab readers, but above all, their writers must not promise more than the story delivers or readers will feel cheated. Furthermore, any hard news in the story has to come soon after that introductory "hook," or be lost in the underbrush.

STRAYED TIME ELEMENT

News writers, concerned about the time the news occurs, must get those two elements, time and action, together, or risk confusion. Usually the time works best just after the verb. Placing the main action verb and time element close together should come naturally. But stories appear every day which leave readers to guess about the time. Here's an example:

> Gov. Arnold Swanson left by plane with four advisers on a trade trip to Japan *Friday*. They will arrive in Tokyo for three days of discussion *Monday*.

If the plane *left Friday* and will *arrive Monday*, each of those two sets of words should appear together. Otherwise, readers may suppose that the plane will arrive on Friday and that three days of discussion somehow will be compressed into one day. This problem of time placement becomes even more critical when the timing of action involves the reader.

> *Tuesday*, Board Chairman Brad Orley announced, all county real estate tax installments will be due by the 6 p.m. deadline.

That happens regularly, to the exasperation of readers who can't tell whether the announcement or the deadline is on Tuesday.

SECOND-DAY LEADS

News has a short shelf life. Many years ago newspapers could "cycle" stories through most editions of a 24-hour period before updating them. That has changed because of a faster pace of events and competition from broadcast media. Today only minutes pass after an announcement or development before reporters have dug up a reaction to it. So the old term "second-day," although still applied to freshened leads and stories, might more accurately be called "second-hour."

This rapid changing of stories puts pressure on reporters and editors to keep up with developments and keep their stories fresh. It's important, though, to give new developments or reactions no more position and perspective than they merit. A story that allows an important development to be buried amid a shower of reaction doesn't serve the reader well.

Sports stories, especially, seem to get tangled easily in second-day reactions and quotes, their authors forgetting to report such important facts as the final score. Afternoon newspapers, delivering their product so many hours after evening contests, emphasize comment and "color," reasoning that radio and television have taken the edge off the hard news. That's a fair assumption, but readers still deserve a good helping of basic reporting.

Readers will consider fraudulent a lead that even hints of subjects to appear later in the story, then doesn't deliver all of them. Such stories are as incomplete as any other story with holes. They come from reporters who don't bother to review their own words. A lead that refers to a "14-point proposal" or "seven-step transition" is a sham if the story doesn't at least outline everything promised.

OLD, TIRED FORMULAS

Because the old "inverted pyramid" lead has declined in importance, only the variety of stories and the innovativeness of writers now limit lead techniques. *The story's news should provide the key to the technique.* Lead writing especially can't follow formulas. Formula writing produces dull stories. Each lead that follows a formula reads too much like one the reader has seen before. It turns an audience off because it simply looks old and tired.

Transition Faults

All writing, from movie scripts to music, must give the audience a helping hand and bring it along with the author. Where would a movie audience be without that stock shot of a jetliner taking off or landing, without that familiar footage of a hotel name or ranch gate? Those scenes "move" the audience along with the story.

Newspaper readers, too, need help in following a news story to keep them from falling off at sharp turns. Today's stories are longer and more complex than yesterday's, involving more people and greater time spans. Readers don't have a screen to show them people and scenes, to show them even whether it's night or day.

Writers must recognize that the audience wasn't at the accident scene or press conference. Unless writers tell them, readers don't know *who* did what, *who* spoke the words and *when* events occurred in relation to other events. They must keep audiences abreast of *place* as well whenever events in a story move from one site to another. These signposts of *person*, *place* and *time* are called *transition*. Other transitions can help by connecting thoughts, by comparing or contrasting ideas. Punctuation, words, phrases, or whole sentences can do it for us.

Transition in Quotation

Quotation marks that continue into the next paragraph, for example, make it clear that the words have been uttered by the same person.

> "These proposals lack support and validity because they don't address the nation's problems.
>
> "If my opponents can't focus on issues before the electorate, a debate is the only solution," Peters said.

Transition in Identity

Proper names, repeated as in the final words above, supply readers with identification. Pronouns of all description work nearly as well in keeping an audience on track.

> Johnson said *he* ran to a nearby house after the collision and called for an ambulance for Mrs. Johnson. *He* said *he* remembers pulling *her* from the wreckage before *he* collapsed.

Transition in Place

Keeping readers aware of *where* events occur may mean using place names once, then using more general terms.

> Ambulances took the three injured persons to Wildwood Memorial Hospital. *There* police questioned Johnson about his route between *the bar* and *the intersection* where the accident occurred.

Transition in Time

Reporters use precise *times* wherever relevant, then rely on words like these to show sequence.

after	earlier	later
afterward	first	meanwhile
before	following	next
during	last	then

Here's an example.

> Johnson said he visited two bars *during the afternoon* and *then* bought a bottle of brandy *before* picking up his friends.

Transition in Ideas

Here are words often used to bridge or to contrast between ideas.

besides	moreover
consequently	nevertheless
finally	on the contrary
for example	on the other hand
furthermore	otherwise
however	therefore
in addition	thus
likewise	

Here's an example.

> *Besides*, he said, the electorate needs ideas before choosing among candidates. He indicated, *however*, that only he has suggested a debate.

Failure in Transition

If a writer omits even a part of this transitional glue readers can lose their grip on strings of continuity that give a story sense and flow. A story hits a slippery slope whenever a transitional gap forces a reader to stop and wonder "Who said that?" or "When did that happen?"

Careless news writers sometimes fail to make clear who's speaking. When a story includes the words of several people, each speaker's name must precede that person's words or come very soon after they begin. Here's an example of faulty speaker transition.

> "Anybody who thinks groundwater pollution can be cleaned up in this valley inside of ten years just isn't being realistic," Jones said.
>
> "Whenever I hear from environmental officials in Washington it gets me all upset again," Hall said. "I wish they'd leave us alone."

As written, that second paragraph appears to be a further quotation from Jones. Then the writer surprises us with another name, Hall, which should have appeared at the beginning of that last paragraph.

Any long, complicated story that includes quotes from several people will be easier to comprehend if the writer occasionally includes both first and last names of sources, and even reminders of their roles.

Another slip in transitional identification isn't so common, but is just as unnerving to readers. This fault makes it appear that a new actor has been introduced when in fact it's the same person.

> Mayor Ivan Johnson's top adviser promised the city council Thursday that the Park Department would disclose its budget deficit. But Deputy City Attorney Ron Adams demanded that his office be allowed to restructure the department without interference.

Readers eventually may conclude that Adams *is* the mayor's adviser, but that kind of construction can leave them befuddled and annoyed.

16

Story Problems

There was a writer named Bing,
Who wanted his phrases to sing.
He trained them, this fella,
To perform a cappella,
But his facts came out ding-a-ling.

Tying Into the Story

Once the lead is out of the way it would seem that a writer should get naturally into the body of a story. But many of today's stories grow out of attractive narrative leads designed more to entice readers than to load them with information. They may put readers into a scene without explaining much of the traditional who, what, when, where or why. Other stories include strings of complexities. Somehow, each writer must form a paragraph to gather them together.

The Nut Graph

A nut graph organizes news in perspective and sets an audience on course. This paragraph is a marriage of orientation and transition. This is an example.

Two cars pulled silently into an alley beside a garage where one window showed a dim light.

Eight dark figures slid from the cars. Four moved to an

overhead door on the alley side of the garage and the others converged at a smaller door nearest the cars. A command followed a kick that smashed the door frame:

"Everybody on the floor, now! This is a bust!"

It was 8:30 p.m. on Friday, March 14. The county's narcotics intervention squad had arrested a five-member "drug family" in the eastern bottoms.

Without that nut graph, the story has no premise or direction.

Tie-backs

Compare a daily newspaper with about 50 serialized books. The newspaper puts a page from each of those books in readers' hands every day and asks them to keep every story in perspective. Some stories depend so much on what has happened already that they can create confusion unless writers build bridges to previous developments.

Word bridges, called *tie-backs,* should help an audience make the connections. Done well, they achieve perspective without getting in the way.

> Councilman Sam Smith offered a plan Friday to get city garbage haulers into recycling paper, plastics and glass.
>
> Smith's proposal *would mesh with the program approved by voters June 9 making recycling mandatory by all Lincoln-wood residents. That program made no provision for organized collection.*

Readers usually remember few details of earlier stories, especially those more than a week old. Without the tie-back in the paragraph above an audience would feel lost trying to judge the effect of the latest development. Sources don't automatically tell reporters how their words, actions and ideas fit into what already has happened. It's the news writer's responsibility to ask the questions and search the records.

Similarly, many of today's stories have ties to the future. Reporters never know precisely what will happen as a result of today's development. But so many stories connect to known schedules of government and institutional bodies that reporters who make the effort can find the next date for consideration.

> Return of Native American artifacts to Lakota tribal leaders won approval Tuesday from the state Historical Society.
>
> Tribal officers could not be reached for comment but have pressed the state to clear its museums of skeletons and grave materials. The *next tribal meeting will be at 7 p.m. Tuesday in the Millville council hall where the society's action likely will be discussed.*

Interpretation of Facts

Although reporters don't put their own opinions into news stories they can solicit the opinions of true authorities regarding the implications of developments. They can also provide readers accurate information on what has happened previously under similar circumstances.

> Every farmer owning land along Snowy River below Loving Reservoir will be subject to a new water use tax under a law signed Friday by Gov. George Andrews.
>
> This was the fourth legislation in seven years directed at recovering a part of reservoir costs from land owners. *The state Supreme Court in each instance has struck down similar legislation as unconstitutional because it can't be applied fairly.*
>
> *Atty. Gen. Jim Squires suggested in an informal opinion Friday afternoon that the court could accept a challenge suit within two months and would reject the latest law as it had the other four.*

Holes in Stories

A news story is incomplete when readers can't find answers to their questions. It has failed to do its job because the writer has failed, either to ask the questions in getting the story, or to include the answers in writing it. Audiences are shortchanged and may question why they buy the newspaper.

A story, for example, may tease a reader with information that baseball players who miss three practice sessions will get smaller paychecks. The first questions in a reader's mind are "which players?" and "how much?" as well as "how often does this happen?"

Another story reports that a university president will receive an annual pay increase of $3,000 next year. The story is incomplete if it doesn't include the president's present salary and percentage of increase. It ought to compare the salary with that of presidents at similar institutions and compare the percentage with other university increases so readers will have necessary background. That goes beyond information released by university regents, but scrambling for facts is part of good reporting and good writing.

When a story tells about plans by a city or county to eliminate offices or services to reduce the budget, reporters have to ask the questions and do their homework: How much will this cut taxes for a home owner? If service cuts won't result in lower taxes, why not? How many people will lose their jobs? What will happen to the office space? Is similar service available elsewhere, and is it more or less expensive if offered by private business?

Sentences That Lose Reader Interest

A reader can bail out in mid-sentence unless the reporter keeps the hook deeply imbedded and *pulling*. A direct, strong sentence assures that best. Most often it starts with a subject and ends with a verb.

> **Weak:** Sam Smith was shot in the hand by his wife, Mary, but his finger was sewn on again by Dr. William Carr.
>
> **Strong:** Dr. William Carr retrieved a finger from the floor, sewed it back on Sam Smith's hand, then discovered that Sam's wife had shot it off.

Too Many Passive Verbs

Weakness in the example above comes partly from *passive* verbs. Unless they check their verbs in every sentence writers can pick up the passive bug, which spreads like a disease around a newsroom. Most news people know that passive verb forms weaken writing, but they don't work hard enough to keep them out of their stories. Compare these examples.

> **Passive:** The council *was given* five days to approve the ordinance before homeowners *would be allowed* to leave their pets run free.
>
> **Active:** Hansen said the council *must approve* the ordinance within five days or private pets legally *can run* free.

Verbs Are Strong, Adjectives Weak

It's easy but ineffective for a writer to throw in adjectives or adverbs in describing a person, scene or action for audiences. Modifiers usually limit or qualify, requiring interpretation by each reader. Action verbs describe better by helping to paint accurate pictures in readers' minds.

> **Weak:** The town's dreary main street *was* uninhabited except for a sleepy dog that *lay* in the dust of one doorway.
> **Strong:** Dust and solitude *controlled* the town's main street, *occupied* only by a dog that *sought* sleep in a doorway.

A writer looking for strong verbs should stay away from forms of the verb *to be,* including *it is, there is, there are,* etc. Those verbs don't cut or dart, they simply *are,* requiring a modifier to give them a sign of life.

> **Weak:** Progress in developing a recycling program *was slow* after Christmas.
> **Strong:** Progress in developing a recycling program *slackened* after Christmas.

Writers shouldn't try so hard to avoid *is* or *was,* however, that they fall into the habit of using *served as* or *worked as* in describing a person's occupation, as in, "She *worked as* a nurse." That sounds as if she isn't qualified, somehow. Write it simply, "She *was* a nurse."

Lack of Specifics

Closely observed and reported detail brings a story to life. Besides providing information, details let readers appreciate the writer's, and newspaper's work. Even so, writers must choose carefully among details. Unneeded facts only fill space and make a story dull. Choosing vague, indefinite words rather than specific ones leaves readers only partly satisfied and wondering why they bothered.

> **Vague:** The bridge lay within a few miles of town.
> **Precise:** The bridge lay on Highway 2, 10 miles east of town.

Vague: The ordinance provides for new paving on parts of Hitchcock Street and most of Wendland Avenue.

Precise: The 14 blocks of Hitchcock between Oak and Spruce will get new paving, as well as 19 blocks of Wendland from Morissey to the city limits.

Vague: Warden Holmes said the three, who escaped three weeks ago, were captured Tuesday in Iowa.

Precise: Warden Holmes said the three escaped March 4th. He said Sioux City, Iowa, police captured them in a park at noon Tuesday.

Vague: Johnson said his opponent deserves defeat because he "insulted" several women in the secretarial pool at his office.

Precise: Johnson said his opponent deserves defeat because he regularly addressed two secretaries in his office as "honey."

Try Showing, Not Telling

It's just as important to be real as to be precise. For comprehension and interest, *concrete* words, which present things and actions familiar to readers, are always more effective than *abstract* terms. Abstract terms involve thoughts or concepts of quality without providing an example.

The abstract concept *beauty* seems simple enough, but nobody can define it without offering a concrete example. Readers will think, "Beauty as compared to what?" It often helps to tell them what a thing or situation is *like*. Comparisons ought to be accurate and within the experience of most readers.

Abstract: Visitors at the rose show could wander for blocks among beautiful buds and blossoms.
Concrete: Blossoms at the rose show ranged from baby-face pink to fire-engine red.

Abstract: Gorgeous clouds moved in from the coast at about dusk.
Concrete: Clouds at dusk swirled upward like whipped ice cream on a cone.

Abstract: One of the inspectors smoked a cigar with a terrible odor.
Concrete: One inspector smoked a cigar that workers said smelled like burning garbage and made them ill.

Abstract: In 1944 the city of Tunis was drab, smelly and full of trash.
Concrete: In 1944 the war had turned the city of Tunis into an overturned garbage can.

For an audience to _sense_ (see, smell, hear, taste or feel) the action and scene, a good writer provides the right words to trip little switches in each reader's memory of common experiences. For example, instead of writing

Johnson, the team's 6-foot, 9-inch center, finds it difficult entering regular doorways and sleeping in regular beds.

It would be more natural and effective to write

Johnson, the team's center, had to duck his head at every doorway and sleep doubled up in bed.

17

Humanizing the News

There was a writer named Hughes,
Who thought he had nothing to lose.
He was fired. It's sad.
He learned that it's bad
To confuse his views with the news.

Where Are the *People?*

Stories that deal with *things* seem to fill the pages of newspapers every day. From them, audiences learn about new traffic signals, legislative schedules, power lines knocked down by a storm, proposals to protect an endangered bird and the latest school board budget. Trouble is, in so many of them readers have a difficult time finding themselves, even their interests.

For example, unless a story tells why the city needs new traffic signals for safety, what they cost the taxpayers and how they will affect the time it takes to get to work, it has ignored the reader. Unless another story provides estimates on how much the storm damage will cost and when power can be restored, it's full of words, not information.

Every news story should be regarded as a *people* story. That often means thinking about causes and effects of the latest development. People do things and make or break things. People are government and politics. They form the issues. If writers and editors can't find a way to make a *thing* story into a *people* story, they should kill it as non-news.

Humanizing detail almost always becomes valuable when one writes about people. Readers can switch to television in a moment, where they can *see* people involved in the news. Quoting people in the news provides a critical part of the writing effort, but only a part. Humanizing means making the people in stories real, making them believable, letting the reader "see" them. It means making a reader say, "I know how that person feels and thinks."

Writers give people in the news a presence and believability by letting them tell their own stories wherever possible. To be most effective they sometimes even let readers see what the person was *doing*.

> "You won't see many bulls as friendly as old 'Pinky,'" Greene said, pointing a tattered glove toward a horned roan next to the fence.
> Greene bent to detach a burr from his left sock.
> "I'd give anything to keep from selling the old boy, but folks at the bank say they need a payment next week."

Overloaded Sentences

Don't burden an individual sentence with more length or weight than it can carry. Writers need compound and complex sentences at times to create the necessary associations among ideas and actions, but length strains readers. Good writers who have to use a long, involved sentence try to make the next one short. This kind of pacing gives readers a lift.

> Legislative district reorganization started last year when three down-state districts that are heavily populated challenged the present boundaries, based on 30,000 population. Twenty counties got involved.

Don't Forget Attribution

Except for facts observable or subject to easy confirmation, reporters must attribute each bit of information in a newspaper story to its source, usually a person or a record. Attribution, while never an assurance of truth, provides reality and authority. At least it gives readers someone to credit or blame.

Source persons are those with authoritative information, either because of their position or from having witnessed a news event. Records attributed in news stories can be any document, even a letter or bill of lading. Most authoritative are those recognized as official and legal by the court system: legislation, laws, ordinances, court orders, wills, property deeds, etc.

Attribution becomes superfluous in reporting events witnessed by many or easily checked, as in the following.

> Fire discovered shortly after midnight gutted the main conference hall at Second Presbyterian Church Tuesday, *Fire Chief Vernon Skowles said.*

When reporting information known only to officials or authorities in charge, however, reporters must tie those revelations to sources.

> Three empty gasoline cans point to arson as the cause of the fire, *Fire Chief Vernon Skowles said.*

Never make a reader guess about attribution. The objective is to link statements directly to persons and wording directly to records.

Don't Bury Quotes

Quotations stand near the top among material that makes

news subjects real and believable. So reporters shouldn't bury subjects' words at the bottom of paragraphs. That destroys much of their effectiveness. Here's an example.

> Cowles came to the meeting carrying two boxes of documents. His aides said they would destroy his opponents' arguments. "These papers will blow the top off the investigation," said his executive assistant, Mary Hansen.

Notice that the quotation becomes much more direct and powerful when it leads the paragraph.

> "These papers will blow the top off the investigation," said Cowles' executive assistant, Mary Hansen. She referred to two boxes of documents the industrialist carried into the meeting.

Make Quotations Accurate

Any words appearing inside quotation marks should be those of the source. Altering statements, however slightly, shatters respect for a reporter and credibility for a newspaper. Imagine a reader's reaction to quoted statements in a newspaper that vary from those heard on television.

When a reporter or editor finds it necessary to paraphrase a source's words for any reason, it's also necessary to remove the quotation marks and make the statement an indirect quote.

Say It, Don't Relate It

When presenting a spoken statement from an interview or a speech, *said* makes the best attributive verb. Any other verb used in its place ought to be, first, accurate, and second, necessary. Reporters appear to worry more than readers about the repetition of *said,* and their efforts at variation have produced these absurdities.

> Flames burned through three layers of ceiling before they could be contained, the chief *marveled*.

> Three ladder companies and a truck company responded to the alarm within six minutes, he *interjected*.

> The Fire Department budget needs to be expanded to provide for more firefighters on third shift, he *demanded*.

Here are some equally questionable verbs that have appeared in attribution.

questioned	inquired	grinned
related	ordered	agreed
muttered	claimed	enunciated
opined	explained	

Avoid the attributive words *according to,* which carry a tiny connotation of doubt or disbelief.

Reporters should keep in mind that a source *adds* every bit of information after the first statement. Readers understand that, so it's redundant to use the word *added* in attribution. The same caution applies to *also said*.

The Continuing Present

Whenever a source refers to action that continues or a condition that is still true, be careful to maintain the present tense when paraphrasing. Too many writers and publications revert to past tense when reporting the present. For example, if the source said, "I don't know," paraphrase it, *He said he doesn't know,* and not, *He said he didn't know.*

Too Many and Poor Quotes

Good quotations add life and reality to news stories, but that shouldn't encourage reporters to use every quoted word they have in their notes. Paragraph after paragraph of quotations grow tiresome, especially if they don't add much information.

Experienced reporters can say it better than most of their sources. They can save space, too, summarizing in one paragraph information which might otherwise take three or four. They should use only the best and brightest quoted material from notes taken at speeches or interviews. If the rest adds information it ought to be paraphrased between the paragraphs of quotations. Reporters then should throw out any that can't pass the test of news.

Logical Development and Context

Consider story *logic* and *context* together because each supports the other. Every sentence and paragraph after the story lead ought to build with some order on the lead's information and premise. That means keeping developments in straight lines and steering the story away from side trips and dead ends. A writer shouldn't find it difficult to keep the progression logical in writing stories about occurrences that involve a sequence of events. After the lead, it's natural to put down one action after another in logical progression. It would almost challenge a writer to get matters out of context.

It's another matter when reporters must handle long speeches and complex interviews, especially those involving several sources.

We must assume that speakers deliver speeches logically and in context. In reporting them, however, reporters can scatter material illogically and far from its original context unless they take care with their notes. Copy editors, because they didn't hear the speech, can only question the association of parts that don't make sense. Tape recorders and copies of original speech texts have simplified problems of writing about speeches, but in politics especially, speakers still often allege that their words have been led astray, changing their meaning.

Because reporters take so many interviews on the run and in conjunction with other interviews, they must take notes meticulously. News conference bustle can prevent the use of tape recorders, challenging even the best reporter to keep context straight, let alone sources and their precise words. Without precision, however, quotations are useless.

Positive or Negative?

Good writers usually find that their words cut more cleanly and more effectively if they rephrase negative statements into positive ones where possible, taking care to preserve accuracy. Here are some examples.

> **Negative:** The sheriff's deputy reported that nobody had been killed in the five-car pile-up.
> **Positive:** All 27 drivers and passengers survived the five-car pile-up, the sheriff's deputy said.

> **Negative:** The candidate said he didn't want to disregard his opponent's charges against him.
> **Positive:** The candidate said he wanted to face his opponent's charges.

Lack of Unity

Writers easily fall into the error of allowing their writing style to wander. For example, they may start by using third person nouns or pronouns and switch without thinking to second person.

> Inexperienced *woodworkers* first should check boards available to *them* against lists of materials. Then organize the tools that will be needed for the project. Nothing is worse than discovering after *you've* started that *you* will need more lumber or more tools.

Readers find it even more disturbing to find that verbs in a story or article have changed tense in mid-stride, awkwardly and without warning. After deciding on a principal verb tense for a story, any writer ought to be able to change tense smoothly for a moment where necessary within a sentence.

> Johnson *said* that his plans include going to Chicago where he *will enroll* in a business college.

Most straight news stories appear in past tense, so unity suffers in cases like this.

> Adams *took* the wrong turn at the Elmwood corner and *wound up* east of the river. He *tries* to take a map with him whenever he *drives* alone since that trip.

Changing a story's tone or mood also can shock a reader's sense of concord. Some stories accept a chatty, light-hearted approach. A more formal style works better for others. But few stories can survive abrupt internal mood changes, as if the writer hasn't decided what kind of article to write. Readers may not know what happened, but it leaves them feeling uncomfortable.

> "Nobody bothers me back here in the woods," Sam said, cleaning his tobacco-stained knife on his shirt. "I talk to the squirrels, and when food runs low, I can usually find a tourist who has extra coffee and sugar." He giggled as he spat

> through the open doorway.
>
> The state Department of Human Services announced Friday that it has never counted all the people who live as squatters on public land.

For that matter, every paragraph in a story should maintain its own unity of subject for proper cohesion. Newspaper paragraphs rarely run long enough to cause problems, but writers should watch that second or third sentence to guard against introducing a new topic. In this example the writer should have started a new paragraph for the farm information.

> Highways in the western third of the state became snow-packed within hours, and the Safety Patrol reported that the occupants of nine cars were stranded at one service station. *Farmers and ranchers in the area were reported to be delighted at the promise of increased moisture.*

It Needs an Ending

Several developments have influenced changes in story structure. At one time dedication to what journalists called the inverted pyramid dictated how nearly every story went together. When newspapers delivered to readers their first accounts of any event, all the most important news went into the first paragraph and from that point information entered the story in order of descending importance. The story ended abruptly, sometimes awkwardly, after presenting the last and least element.

The inverted pyramid form also fit the requirements of newspaper page composition when editors couldn't plan pages as closely as they do with computers. A story form that left the least for last allowed page compositors to drop off as much of any story as was necessary for it to fit an opening in the page.

Newspaper readers today often have heard or seen brief

reports of many events. Today's production computers make it possible to plan pages to the last line. These developments have liberated writers, who now can create a form for any story. Among other advantages, that means more imaginative introductions—and real endings.

An ending that concludes smoothly will leave readers more satisfied than one that stops abruptly. One useful technique for endings summarizes the story's point or "what it says." Another technique leaves a poignant or revealing quotation for last, giving the reader a final bite to chew on. Another technique considers the story a circular route that brings an audience back to the starting point as a reminder of the story's central issue. Still another paints a scene of continuing action, reminding readers that they have had only a brief encounter. Whatever the technique, a writer who tries for a smooth way to end the story will help to satisfy readers.

Unless the writer qualifies as a "news analyst," no technique should include any of the writer's opinion. After hours of hard work it's tempting for reporters to leave readers with some of their own impressions and attitudes. But good writers will resist the urge to put some of themselves in the last few lines. Nothing can cancel hard work more effectively. Readers don't care what a news writer thinks.

18

Spelling

There was this writer, Mei Ling,
Who never developed her spelling.
Advised to perfect it,
She chose to neglect it
And had to go into selling.

Heal Thyself

Writers can mislay the letters of words like the bricks of a building. Poor spelling gives away an untrained or careless writer every time. Nothing can hide those broken, mangled elements that editors and readers take almost universally as a mark of illiteracy. Word blunderers have always invented excuses, and although the publishing world may sympathize briefly, nobody who writes much has found a substitute for learning to spell. Editors and readers raise the cry every day: "Doesn't anybody care any more?" Those who have been frustrated and embarrassed can't escape the overwhelming truth: Ailing patients must heal themselves.

Some writers say they learned to spell in the same way they learned to read, by word recognition. They say they follow spelling rules, but improve largely by constant reading, which reinforces their sense of how a word looks when it's spelled right. They suspect a spelling when it doesn't *look* right, claiming a talent especially useful for a copy editor. These people seem to have an advantage, but even they must memorize some spellings and reach for dictionaries to check their sense.

Other people say they follow the rules but rely heavily on sounding out syllables as they did when they learned to read. How a word "sounds" isn't always a good base for its spelling, however. These writers tend to memorize a bit more than others and keep a dictionary within reach.

Still others say that no "system" works well for them. They live with dictionaries and computerized spelling checkers, habitually submitting to authority.

Spelling appears to be more a matter of learning than teaching. Teachers and journalists have quarrelled uselessly among themselves about methods and the proper time and setting for learning to spell. The only solid answers seem to be *always* and *everywhere.* Even after years of good elementary and secondary school training, anyone interested in a life of writing and editing can never abandon the study of language.

A major cause of spelling problems lies in the English language itself. Other languages follow more consistent rules for building, spelling and pronouncing words. What other tongue offers at least seven pronunciations for the four-letter combination *ough?* (dough, bought, bough, hiccough, rough, cough and through)

Despite all this, and conceding that English spelling rules have lists of exceptions, the rules can save a writer time and energy in looking up some words.

Following is a compilation of the most useful guidelines.

1. The suffix *-able* appears at the end of root words that can stand alone. Also, if the root word ends in a single *e,* omit it in most cases before adding *-able.* A couple of exceptions are *changeable* and *noticeable.*

The suffix *-able* always follows the root word ending in *g, i* and the hard *c.*

amiable, revocable, navigable

The suffix spelled *-ible* is less common but often appears after double consonants, *s*, *st*, and the soft *c*.

horrible, plausible, edible, forcible

2. Place the *i* before *e* except after *c* or when sounded with a hard *a*, as in *weigh* or *neighbor*.

achieve, belief, believe, brief, chief, field, fiend, grief, niece, piece, priest, relief, shield, series, siege, species, wield, yield.

Examples of *ei* spellings after *c:*

ceiling, conceit, deceit, perceive, receive

Common exceptions to the rule:

either, leisure, seize, weird, height, heir, their, foreign, sleight

Examples of *ei* spellings which are pronounced with the hard *a* sound:

eight, freight, heinous, neigh, reign, rein, seine, sleigh, veil, vein

3. Before adding a suffix that begins with a vowel (*-ing, -ed, -er, -est, -ish,* etc.) double the final consonant only if it is preceded by a single vowel *and* if the consonant is part of a single syllable or in a word accented on the last syllable.

occurred, occurring, dragged, dragging, quizzed, quizzing, omitted, omitting

Under this rule, words accented on an earlier syllable will not double their final consonant when adding a suffix.

canceling, traveling, profiting

4. If a word ends in a silent *e*, drop the *e* before a suffix that begins with a vowel, but keep the *e* if the suffix begins with a consonant.

Examples of dropping the *e* before a vowel suffix:

arranging, changing, desiring, forcing, guidance, imaginable, lovable, usable

Keeping the *e* before a suffix that begins with a consonant:

arrangement, excitement, fateful, staleness, solely

Exceptions:

shoeing, hoeing, eyeing, mileage

Also *dyeing, singeing, tingeing* retain the *e* to distinguish them from similar words.

5. Before adding endings to words ending in -*y* preceded by a consonant, change the *y* to *i* unless the suffix begins with *i*.

mercy: merciful   study: studying

Words ending in -*y* preceded by a vowel regularly keep the *y* before adding an ending:

relay: relayed   delay: delaying

Some exceptions:

lay: laid   say: said   slay: slain

6. Choosing between the spellings *ede* and *eed* should be easy. Only five words require the double *e*: *deed, exceed, indeed, proceed* and *succeed*.

7. Only six commonly used words end in *-ery* (*cemetery, confectionery, distillery, millinery, monastery* and *stationery*), so they should not be confused with words ending in *ary*.

8. Only four commonly used words end in *-efy* (*liquefy, putrefy, rarefy* and *stupefy*), so they should not be confused with words ending in *-ify*.

9. Nouns usually include the letter *c* where the verb form uses an *s*: *advice* (n), *advise* (v); *prophecy* (n), *prophesy* (v). At least two words are spelled alike for either purpose: *license, practice*.

10. The rules for creating plurals and possessives are covered in Chapter 7.

11. To avoid confusing compound nouns with compound verbs, remember that compound verbs that can be confused usually are two words. The matching compound nouns are one word.

Verb Form	Noun Form
sell out	sellout
spell down	spelldown
run away	runaway
clean up	cleanup
stand by	standby
take off	takeoff

Appendix I: **Words to Memorize**

Some English words defy any spelling rules yet devised and must be memorized, that is, practiced until they can't possibly be misspelled. Many modern educational theories have de-emphasized rote memory exercises, but the memory system offered here has helped hundreds of poor spellers to gain confidence.

The method consists simply in repeated typing of a difficult word at a typewriter or word processor, combining two senses, sight and touch, as the word takes form. Learning to spell a word may mean filling a page or screen with it. Poor spellers can become good spellers, even if they measure progress three or four words at a time.

Following is a list of often-misspelled words. Many do not follow the rules, and it would benefit every journalist to memorize them.

aberration	acoustics	already
abet	adherent	analyze
abridgment	admissible	annihilate
abscess	adviser	anoint
abysmal	affidavit	apparatus
accessible	aficionado	Arctic
accommodate	align	asinine
accumulate	all right	assassinate

auxiliary
baccalaureate
bailiff
barbecue
barbiturate
battalion
beige
bellwether
beneficent
benefited
bettor
bivouac
bivouacking
broccoli
caffeine
caliber
calorie
canceled
canister
carburetor
Caribbean
catalogue
cemetery
chaperon
chauffeur
chili
Cincinnati
collectible
colossal
compatible
competent
connoisseur
consensus
consistency
coolly
corduroy
counterfeit
crystallize

czar
dachshund
daffodil
debilitate
deductible
defendant
deify
deluxe
demagogue
descendant
desiccate
despise
deterrent
diaphragm
diarrhea
diesel
dietitian
dilemma
diphtheria
discernible
discipline
dissension
drought
drunkenness
dumbbell
dumfounded
ecstasy
eerie
embarrass
excel
exhilarate
exorbitant
extension
extol
exuberant
Fahrenheit
fiery
firefighter

fluorescent
fluoridate
forfeit
fuchsia
fulfill
furor
fuselage
fusillade
gabardine
gaiety
garnishee
garrulous
gauge
gelatin
genealogy
glycerin
goodbye
gorilla
gray
grievance
gruesome
guarantee
guerrilla
gypsy
habeas corpus
hara-kiri
harass
harebrained
harelip
height
heinous
heir
hemorrhage
hemorrhoids
hiccup
hitchhiker
homicide
hors d'oeuvres

hygiene
hypocrisy
hysterical
illegibly
illegitimate
imminent
impostor
impresario
incandescent
infrared
innocuous
innuendo
inoculate
installment
iridescent
irrelevant
judgment
jujitsu
keenness
kerosene
khaki
kidnapped
kimono
knowledgeable
labyrinth
larynx
legionnaire
leisure
liaison
likable
likelihood
lilies
liquefy
lissome
livable
lovable
maintenance
marijuana

massacre
medieval
mediocre
memento
mileage
minuscule
mischievous
missile
misspell
moccasin
mollify
monastery
mustache
naive
naphtha
nauseous
nickel
numskull
obbligato
obeisance
occurrence
oculist
omniscient
pantomime
paraffin
parallel
paraphernalia
pari-mutuel
pasteurize
pastime
pavilion
peaceable
penicillin
peremptory
persevere
personnel
pharmaceutical
phenomenon

Philippines
phlegm
picnicking
pinochle
Pittsburgh
plagiarism
plebiscite
poignant
poinsettia
potpourri
powwow
prerogative
propellant
propeller
prurient
pygmy
quandary
querulous
queue
raccoon
rarefied
raveling
reconnaissance
recur
relevant
religious
renaissance
repellent
resistant
restaurateur
resuscitate
reveille
rhapsody
rheumatism
rhythm
ricochet
saboteur
saccharin

sacrilegious
salable
sanatorium
sanitarium
secession
seize
separate
sergeant
sheriff
shillelagh
siege
sieve
signaled
silhouette
sizable
skeptic
skiing
sleight-of-hand
soliloquy
soluble
somersault
sophomore
souffle
souvenir
sovereign
specter
spiraled
straitjacket

stratagem
stupefy
sulfur
supersede
surfeit
surveillance
sycophant
symmetry
synagogue
syphilis
taffeta
tariff
teen-age
temblor
temperamental
tendency
tepee
till
toboggan
tonsillitis
toupee
traipse
tranquillity
traveler
Tucson
turbulent
tyrannous
ukulele

usable
vacillate
vacuum
verifiable
vermilion
versatile
vicissitude
vilify
villain
Wednesday
weird
wholly
wield
wiener
willful
wiry
withhold
wondrous
woolly
X-ray
yield
yogurt
zany
zigzag
zinc
zoology
zucchini

Appendix II: A Stylebook Summary

Rules of English punctuation, capitalization, spelling, abbreviation and numerals have never come to us etched in stone. We have only guidelines from a multitude of "authorities." No publication can continue more than a few days without its editors asking themselves, "Whose rules will we follow?" They need a formal *style*.

They have recognized that every paragraph brings questions of correctness, not only to satisfy the desire for acceptability, but the desire for *consistency*.

Publications seek consistency to help them gain and hold credibility. For example, if a newspaper were to treat the name *Vietnam* as one word in one story and as two words in another, readers might reasonably question the paper's reliability and dependability. Consistency builds a reader's "comfort" level.

At one time editors of every publication developed their own "stylebook," usually a booklet of guidelines for consistency. The best and most practical of these gradually became adopted by other publications. The Associated Press and United Press International together developed a comprehensive stylebook for wire service consistency, and most newspapers have adopted it for their own general use. Each newspaper typically adds its own rules covering local proper names and other special cases.

This wire service stylebook is a volume in itself, so only

those rules of style most commonly used will be summarized here. Anyone who writes regularly for newspapers should learn them. Chapter 6 on punctuation covers those rules.

Abbreviations and Acronyms

Avoid general use of either abbreviations or acronyms unless they are universally recognized, clear from the context or required by the circumstance.

1. Titles With Names

On first reference before a full name abbreviate these titles if they are outside direct quotations: *Dr., Gov., Lt. Gov., Rep., the Rev.* and military titles. Drop the title in subsequent references. Do not abbreviate Attorney General, District Attorney, President, Professor and Superintendent.

Do not use courtesy titles (*Mr., Mrs., Miss, Ms.*) except to avoid confusion between husband and wife in second reference. Retain them also in direct quotations.

Abbreviate Jr. and Sr. where appropriate after names and do not set them off with commas.

2. Organizations

Write out the full name the first time, except for such well-known organizations as CIA, FBI and GOP. After first reference use the acronym. Never use the abbreviation in parenthesis after the name on first reference.

Abbreviate *Co., Cos., Corp., Inc.* and *Ltd.* after the company name, even if the formal names spells it in full. Do not abbreviate these words if other words follow them. Abbreviate *Co., Cos., Corp.* even if followed by *Inc.* or *Ltd.*

Never abbreviate the word *association,* even if part of a name.

Abbreviate political affiliation this way after a name: Rep. Sam Smith, D-Ariz.

3. Dates

Days of the week are always spelled out.

Names of months with five letters or fewer (March, April, May, June, July) are never abbreviated. Abbreviate the others only when the month is accompanied by the date of the month: *Oct. 12, 1992.*

Write out *Fourth of July.*

Never abbreviate *Christmas* as *Xmas.*

4. Symbols

$—Use before figures. Write the word *dollar* only in abstract references to values, amounts, etc.

¢—Write out *cent* or *cents.*

%—Write out *percent.*

&—Write out *and,* except where the abbreviation is part of an organization's name.

5. Place Names

Spell out a state name unless it comes after one of the state's towns or cities: *Nebraska; Larned, Kan.* Also, never abbreviate *Alaska, Hawaii* or any state with fewer than five letters: *Idaho, Iowa, Maine, Ohio, Texas, Utah.*

Use the following state abbreviations instead of the two-letter style of the post office.

Ala.	Kan.	Neb.
Ariz.	Ky.	Nev.
Calif.	La.	N.H.
Colo.	Md.	N.J.
Conn.	Mass.	N.M.
Del.	Mich.	N.Y.
Fla.	Minn.	N.C.
Ga.	Miss.	N.D.
Ill.	Mo.	Okla.
Ind.	Mont.	Ore.

Pa.	Tenn.	W.Va.
R.I.	Vt.	Wis.
S.C.	Va.	Wyo.
S.D.	Wash.	

Follow the name of a town or city in the United States with the abbreviation of that state unless the town appears on the stylebook's list of places that are so well known that they need no further identification. Similarly, foreign towns or cities should be followed by the full name of their country unless they are well-known cities that appear on the list.

The words *street, avenue, boulevard* or directional words should be abbreviated only when they appear with specific addresses: *412 California St., 911 S. Sumner Ave.*

Always abbreviate U.S., but never a state's name, if a part of a highway name. Always write out interstate highways on first reference and abbreviate on subsequent references: *Interstate 80, I-80.*

Spell out United States and United Nations as nouns but abbreviate as *U.S.* and *U.N.* as adjectives.

Never abbreviate *Fort* or *Mount. Saint* is abbreviated *St.* in place names, with these exceptions: *Saint* John, New Brunswick; Sault *Ste.* Marie, Mich. (and Ontario).

6. Punctuating Abbreviations

Use periods to punctuate most abbreviations of two letters or fewer: U.S., U.N., N.D., A.D., B.C., St., a.m. Some exceptions are AP, AM broadcast, 20mm ammunition, IQ, TV, R-Iowa.

Do not use periods to punctuate most abbreviations with three letters or more: NATO, CIA, FBI, mph, mpg. An exception is c.o.d.

7. Other Abbreviation Rules

Abbreviate and capitalize the word *number* if followed by

a numeral: *No. 34.*

Do not abbreviate *versus* as *v.*

Capitalization

1. Proper Nouns

Generally, capitalize proper nouns but not common nouns. Where proper nouns are parts of names of animals, food and plants, capitalize that part of the name that would be a proper name standing by itself: *English* bulldog, *Welsh* rarebit. Among exceptions are those words which derived from proper names but no longer depend on them for their meaning: *french* fries, *venetian* blind, *manhattan* cocktail.

Where possible, use generic terms instead of trade names which must be capitalized: *facial tissue* instead of *Kleenex*; *gelatin* instead of *Jell-O,* etc.

2. Titles

Capitalize formal titles of people when they appear before a name, but do not capitalize occupational titles: *President* Wilson, *Pope* Clement, *engineer* George Carlson.

3. Regions

Capitalize the names of regions. Do not capitalize directions: He had to drive *south.* He vacationed in the *South.*

Capitalize a region when it appears with a country's name only when it is part of the name: *South* Korea, *north* Scotland. Capitalize a region appearing with a state or city name only when the region is well known and the name well accepted: *South* Bronx, *Southern* California. Capitalize adjectives and nouns which refer to a region: *Southern* hospitality, *Easterners, Northwest* Indians.

4. Shared Plurals

Do not capitalize a word shared by two or more proper nouns: Mission and Mason *streets,* Blue and Minnehaha *rivers.*

5. *Government and Academic*

Always capitalize government departments: *Street Department, Treasury Department.* Do not capitalize college departments except for those words which would be capitalized standing alone: *English* department, *geography* department.

Capitalize academic and government committees only when writing the full, formal name: the Senate *Appropriations Committee.* Do not capitalize shortened versions of a name: *narcotics committee.*

Do not capitalize or abbreviate academic degrees: *bachelor of fine arts degree, master's of science degree.*

Do not capitalize the words *administration, federal* and *government.* Capitalize *president* and *vice president* only when they appear before names. Capitalize *Board of Curators* and *Board of Education,* but not *board of directors* or *board of trustees.*

Capitalize *City Council* and *County Commission,* but make *council* and *commission* lower case when standing alone or when used generically or in plural form. Capitalize *Legislature* and *Cabinet* if they are the formal names of those bodies. The building, *Capitol,* is capitalized, but not the city, *capital.*

Capitalize military titles before names: *Cpl.* Albert Jones, *Gen.* William Smith. When referring to U.S. armed forces capitalize *Air Force, Army, Marines* and *Navy.*

Capitalize political parties, including the word *Party,* when they refer to parties and not to philosophies: *Republican Party, Labor Party, Communist Party, communist, libertarian.*

6. *Racial References*

Capitalize names of races but not colors: *Negro, Caucasian,* black, white.

7. Religious References

Capitalize *God* and *Jesus,* but not their pronouns: *he, his, him.* Capitalize *Mass,* but not *pope* unless it comes before a name. Capitalize *Bible* only when it refers to Holy Scriptures and not another publication: the golfer's *bible.*

8. Quotations

Capitalize the first word of a quotation only if it is within quotation marks and is a complete sentence or complete paragraph.

9. Questions

Capitalize the first word of a question that appears within a sentence: She was bursting to ask, *What* happens next?

Treatment of Numerals

1. Cardinal Numbers

Use numerals to express ages: *68* years old, Sarah Smith, *21*; *3*-month-old Jimmy Jones.

Street addresses should be in numerals: *1712* Smith Ave.

Use numerals alone in dates, without including *-nd, -th* or *-st*: June *21, 1992.*

Use numerals in monetary amounts, but for millions or more use the words *million* or *billion*: *$3.2 million.*

In dimensions: *6* feet tall, *21*-by-*20*-foot room, *80*-foot wingspan. Omit hyphens when the word being described refers to size: *6 feet deep, 8 feet across.*

Always use numerals to express percentages, except at the beginning of a sentence.

To express speeds: *65* mph, *32* knots.

To express the specific time of day: *6:28* p.m. But use the words *noon* and *midnight,* as well as *seven* minutes and *eight* hours.

To express temperature spell out only the word *zero*. Also, spell out the word *minus* except in tables.

Express sports scores, gains, etc., in numerals: *7* to *6, 3*-yard gain, *15*-foot vault.

Express sizes in numerals: *8* AA, *42*-regular, *10* petite.

Highway references: Nebraska *2,* Interstate *80.*

Weight references: *6* pounds, *3* ounces.

Latitude and longitude: *46* degrees, *21* minutes.

2. Numerals With Suffixes -nd, -rd, -st and -th

Use those suffixes in numbering districts, precincts and wards: *4th* Congressional District.

Military and naval ranks or units with numbers: *2nd* Lt., *1st* Armored Division, *2nd* Fleet.

In referring to courts: *2nd* District Court.

Constitutional amendments after the *Ninth*. Spell out numbers of amendments through Ninth.

For streets numbered higher than *Ninth,* but spell out street numbers through Ninth: *12th* St., *Seventh* Ave.

3. Instead of Numerals

Use words for numbers *nine and under.*

Use words for casual expressions like a *thousand* pardons, thanks a *million.*

Use words to express fractions less than one: *one-fourth.*

Use words to start sentences unless the number is a year: *1992* was a good vintage.

Use words instead of numerals to conform to practice in proper names: *Twentieth* Century Fund.

4. Roman Numerals

Kings, queens, popes and world wars, as well as men who are third or later with the same name, can be identified with appropriate Roman numerals: Samuel Arndt *III,* Queen Elizabeth *II,* World War *II.*

Bibliography

Anderson, Douglas A., and Itule, Bruce D. *Writing the News*. New York: Random House, 1988.

Baskette, Floyd K., Sissors, Jack Z., and Brooks, Brian S. *The Art of Editing*. 4th ed. New York: Macmillan, 1986.

Bernstein, Theodore M. *The Careful Writer*. New York: Atheneum, 1977.

_____. *Dos, Don'ts & Maybes of English Usage*. New York: Times Books, 1977.

Bremner, John B. *Words on Words*. New York: Pocket Books, 1965.

Brooks, Brian S., and Pinson, James L. *Working With Words*. New York: St. Martin's, 1989.

Bullions, The Rev. Peter. *Analytical and Practical Grammar*. 36th ed. New York: Farmer, Brace & Company, 1856.

Callihan, E. L. *Grammar for Journalists*, 3d ed. Radnor, Pa.: Chilton, 1979.

Cappon, Rene J. *The Word*. New York: The Associated Press, 1982.

Cochran, William C., and Bevis, Howard L. *Cochran's Law Lexicon*, 3d ed. Cincinnati: W. H. Anderson, 1924.

Copperud, Roy H. *American Usage and Style. The Consensus*. New York: Van Nostrand Reinhold, 1980.

Copple, R. Neale. *Depth Reporting: An Approach to Journalism*. Englewood Cliffs, N.J.: Prentice-Hall, 1964.

Ferguson, Donald L., and Patten, Jim. *Journalism Today!* Chicago: National Textbook Company, 1986.

Flesch, Rudolf. *The ABC of Style*. New York: Harper & Row, 1964.

Flesch, Rudolf. *Look It Up*. New York: Harper & Row, 1977.

Foerster, Norman, and Steadman, J. M., Jr. *Writing and Thinking*.

Revised. New York: Houghton Mifflin, 1941.

Follett, Wilson. *Modern American Usage: A Guide*. Edited by Jacques Barzun. New York: Hill & Wang, 1966.

Fowler, H. W. *A Dictionary of Modern English Usage,* 2d ed. New York: Oxford University Press, 1965.

French, Christopher W., ed. *The Associated Press Stylebook and Libel Manual*. New York: The Associated Press, 1986.

Gilmore, Gene. *Modern Newspaper Editing*. 3d ed. Ames, Iowa: Iowa State University Press, 1984.

Gove, Philip Babcock, ed. *Webster's Third New International Dictionary*. Springfield, Mass.: G.&C. Merriam Co., 1986.

Johnson, Edward D. *Handbook of Good English*. New York: Washington Square Press, 1983.

Kessler, Lauren, and McDonald, Duncan. *When Words Collide,* 2d ed. Belmont, Calif.: Wadsworth, 1988.

Kilpatrick, James J. *The Ear Is Human*. Kansas City, Mo.: Andrews, McMeel & Parker, 1985.

_____. *The Writer's Art*. Kansas City, Mo.: Andrews, McMeel & Parker, 1984.

Lippman, Thomas W., ed. *The Washington Post Deskbook on Style,* 2d ed. New York: McGraw-Hill, 1989.

MacDougal, Curtis D., and Reid, Robert D. *Interpretative Reporting,* 9th ed. New York: Macmillan, 1987.

McMahan, Elizabeth. *A Crash Course in Composition,* 2d ed. New York: McGraw-Hill, 1977.

Miller, Casey, and Swift, Kate. *Handbook of Nonsexist Writing,* 2d ed. New York: Harper & Row, 1988.

Neufeldt, Victoria, and David B. Guralnik, eds. *Webster's New World Dictionary,* 3d College ed. New York: Webster's New World, 1988.

Newman, Edwin. *Edwin Newman on Language: Strictly Speaking* and *A Civil Tongue*. New York: Warner Books, 1980.

Radford, Maude L. *Composition and Rhetoric*. New York: Hinds & Noble, 1903.

Research and Education Association. *The English Handbook of Grammar, Style, and Composition*. New York: Research and Education Association, 1984.

Ryan, Michael, and Tankard, James W., Jr. *Basic News Reporting*. Palo

Alto, Calif.: Mayfield, 1977.

Safire, William. *On Language*. New York: Times Books, 1980.

Strunk, William, Jr., and White, E. B. *The Elements of Style,* 3d ed. New York: Macmillan, 1979.

Swan, Michael. *Practical English Usage*. New York: Oxford University Press, 1981.

Venolia, Jan. *Write Right!* Berkeley, Calif.: Ten Speed Press, 1982.

Zinsser, William. *On Writing Well,* 3d ed. New York: Harper & Row, 1985.

Index